A GUIDE TO FIELD IDENTIFICATION
OF NORTH AMERICAN SPECIES

EASTERN
BIRDS

written and illustrated by
JAMES COE

GOLDEN PRESS • NEW YORK
Golden Books Publishing Company, Inc.
Racine, Wisconsin 53404

FOREWORD

There are millions of birdwatching enthusiasts in America today who enjoy an unprecedented choice of fine references to help them identify obscure species of birds, including comprehensive field guides, detailed regional or state guides, and sophisticated monographs describing particular groups of birds. Surprisingly, though, there are few guides suitable for the novice or casual birdwatcher.

Whether you have been feeding birds in your backyard for years or are strictly a vacation birdwatcher, or whether you have accompanied your spouse or an enthusiastic friend on numerous birdwatching expeditions but haven't yet summoned the courage to venture out on your own, *Eastern Birds* and its companion volume to follow, *Western Birds,* are the perfect guides for you. I believe that no other books currently available can offer as much information in an easy-to-use format while not overwhelming the reader with too many birds and too much detail.

It is a tricky affair—writing an abridged guide. Within the limited space available in each volume, I have tried to include enough species and plumages so that an enterprising beginner will not be confused and frustrated by finding birds that are not in the book. Yet I was determined not to clutter up the pages with exotic rarities that most of us will probably never see. I am sure that there have been some omissions and some inconsistencies. But I hope that the choices I have made work for you.

I want to express my gratitude to the many authors, artists, ornithologists, and photographers whose work I consulted during the years that I worked on this project. I am most indebted to Guy Tudor, whose advice and keen eye improved the plates immeasurably and who also helped me organize the guides and offered much constructive criticism of the text, and to Paul Lehman, who drew upon his vast expertise and field experience to compile the maps and review the text and artwork for accuracy. My thanks to my agent, Harold Roth, editors Maury Solomon and Caroline Greenberg, and art director Remo Cosentino for their wisdom, patience, and faith that I would someday finish the project. Additional thanks to my publishers for their indulgence and supreme patience, to my brother, David Coe, for his help with the first drafts, and to my parents, Sylvia and Jacques, without whom I never could have become a bird artist and field guide author. Finally, thanks to my wife, Karen, whose love and support keep me going every day, and to Jonah, who inspires me as he discovers the world for himself.

J. C.

CONTENTS

INTRODUCTION..4

MASTER PLATES 12

LOONS AND GREBES..26

MISCELLANEOUS SEABIRDS..28

CORMORANTS, ANHINGAS, AND PELICANS 30

WATERFOWL..32

BIRDS OF PREY...44

STORKS, SPOONBILLS, IBISES, AND LIMPKINS............................52

HERONS, EGRETS, AND BITTERNS...54

CRANES...58

GAMEBIRDS...58

RAILS AND GALLINULES...62

PLOVERS...64

SHOREBIRDS 66

GULLS 74

TERNS 78

PIGEONS AND DOVES 82

CUCKOOS AND ALLIES 84

OWLS...86

SWIFTS AND NIGHTJARS 90

HUMMINGBIRDS 92

KINGFISHERS 92

WOODPECKERS 92

FLYCATCHERS...98

SWALLOWS 102

CROWS AND JAYS 104

TITMICE 106

NUTHATCHES AND CREEPERS 108

WRENS..110

MIMIC THRUSHES AND SHRIKES 112

THRUSHES 114

WAXWINGS 116

GNATCATCHERS AND KINGLETS..118

VIREOS 118

WOOD-WARBLERS 122

BLACKBIRDS AND STARLINGS 134

ORIOLES AND TANAGERS...138

GROSBEAKS, BUNTINGS, AND CARDINALS................................140

SPARROWS 142

PIPITS, LARKS, AND MISCELLANEOUS OPEN-COUNTRY FINCHES.......148

FINCHES...150

OLD WORLD SPARROWS...152

APPENDIX 154

INDEX 158

INTRODUCTION

A GUIDE FOR BEGINNERS

Everyone knows the American Robin, with its ruddy breast. Most of us have glimpsed at least once the blue flash of a jay as it streaked by, or have strolled past gulls lined up like sentinels on the beach, or have watched ducks snapping up bread crumbs in the pond at the city park. Birds are a part of our surroundings; we encounter them almost every day. Yet most of us know little about them.

Eastern Birds is specially designed to provide beginning birdwatchers with a fundamental knowledge of birds. This guide offers a novel approach for anyone who has ever wanted to learn more about the birds around us but who has, until now, been discouraged by the dry, technical format of other birdwatchers' field guides.

Most comprehensive North American bird guides are intimidating; they describe nearly every kind of bird that has ever been recorded on the continent (defined here as the United States and Canada). That's over 800 species! In the Golden guide, only those species that are widely distributed on the eastern portion of the continent, or that are common locally, are illustrated and discussed in the text. Birds that are restricted to peripheral areas such as the Florida Keys, Aleutian Islands, Mexican border region, and open ocean have been omitted, as have some of the rarer and more obscure varieties of hawks, sandpipers, flycatchers, and sparrows.

Eastern Birds covers the eastern portion of North America, west to the foothills of the Rocky Mountains and south into Texas, skirting the eastern rim of the Edwards Plateau. Although this guide is abridged and designed to be accessible, it is still thorough. It contains a wealth of material about bird identification, natural history, and ecology. The paintings depict information not usually shown in standard field guides and not necessarily mentioned in the text, including landscapes of a favorite habitat or a species' characteristic behavior.

HOW TO USE THE MASTER PLATES

If you have ever tried to use a conventional bird guide, then you know how frustrating it can be to find your way through page after page of seemingly identical birds. *Eastern Birds* contains an innovative section of Master Plates (pp. 12-25) that will help direct you to the appropriate pages of the book.

The Master Plates are, in effect, a visual index to the rest of the guide. On these pages, unrelated but often confused species are illustrated side by side, usually in a common scene. These birds may share habitat preferences, feeding behavior, and similar shapes or distinguishing field marks, but because they are unrelated, they appear separately in the main text. Each figure on a Master Plate is cross-referenced to the page in the main section of the book where that species and closely related birds are discussed and illustrated in full.

Turn to the Master Plates before you attempt to identify a new bird. Look for an image that resembles the bird you are observing, paying special attention to shape, posture, and other distinguishing marks noted under "Looking at Birds." Then turn to the page indicated next to that figure and continue your search for the species you might have seen. Not every species is represented on a Master Plate, but typical examples of each distinctive group are shown.

HOW TO READ THE RANGE MAPS

In this guide, range maps appear next to the text entries for most species, except those with ranges that can be described clearly in the text. Use these maps to identify at a glance which birds inhabit a specific region of eastern North America. The colored areas of the maps represent a species' distribution. Red indicates its range during the summer breeding season, blue indicates winter range, and purple denotes those areas in which the bird is a permanent resident. Species that migrate during spring and fall may pass over large portions of the continent, stopping to feed in preferred habitats along their path. Migratory ranges are indicated on the maps by vertical lines.

KEY TO THE RANGE MAPS

■ = summer or breeding range

■ = winter range

■ = year-round or permanent range

▥ = occurrence during migration

Keep in mind that the distributions shown are approximate. Only rarely do ranges end as abruptly as the maps suggest. Unless confined by some geographic barrier, a species tends to be most abundant at the core of its range and less common at the edges. However, some birds have spotty distributions throughout their range. American White Pelicans, for example, breed in colonies on islands in just a few lakes of the Central Great Plains, but are absent from other suitable lakes within their mapped range. And Marsh Wrens, although widespread, occur only in marshes with tall reeds and cattails. Such species are said to be *locally common.*

Also keep in mind that birds have wings. While flying, they can be buffeted by storms and swept far outside their usual range, or they may simply become lost. Individuals that show up way out of range are called *vagrants* or *accidentals.* Identifying such rarities requires great care and years of birding experience, but such finds are among the most exciting moments for any birder.

Some bird species are nomadic by nature. Their distribution may vary unpredictably from year to year or during certain seasons. For instance, many species of herons and ibis, especially young birds, undergo *post-breeding dispersal* during late summer and may wander far inland and north of their breeding range. Snowy Owls and certain finches, which nest in the far North, are also known for erratic migrations southward during some winters (known as *irruptions*).

BIRDWATCHING BASICS

Bird Names and Classification. Ornithologists have recognized close to 9,000 different kinds of birds worldwide. Almost 900 species have been identified in North America, and about 650 of these nest on the continent.

Keeping track of this many species requires a system. The highly structured system of classification, or *taxonomy*, devised for this purpose applies to all living creatures, not just to birds. This ordered sequence of species is like a family tree, and it is designed to chart evolutionary history. Ancient and supposedly "primitive" species are followed by more specialized, or "advanced," forms. Some relationships on this family tree are little more than educated guesses; others have been substantiated by the evidence of fossil remains, studies of physiological structure, or a comparison of chemical similarities revealed in DNA studies. The taxonomy is continually refined as researchers learn more about each species and new techniques used in studying these relationships are developed. The names used in this guide are those recognized by the American Ornithologists Union's *Checklist of North American Birds* (6th ed., 1983, and supplements).

In addition to the common name by which each kind of bird is known, every species is assigned a unique two-part name in Latin, called a *binomial*. This scientific name enables ornithologists from any country to refer with certainty to the same biological entity. The name of the genus, which comes first, refers to a group of closely related species. The second, specific name is descriptive of that particular species. For example, the American Robin is known as *Turdus migratorius*, meaning "wandering thrush."

The next higher category is the family, encompassing one or more genera and their component species. This is the level at which birds are usually grouped together in field guides. All woodpeckers, for instance, belong to one family. Within that family, however, the Downy Woodpecker *(Picoides pubescens)* and the Hairy Woodpecker *(Picoides villosus)*, both in the same genus, are more closely related to each other than to the Pileated Woodpecker *(Dryocopus pileatus)*.

Getting Started. Birdwatching requires little equipment. If you have purchased this guide, you are almost ready to get started.

Although you may be able to see birds attracted to a window feeder well enough with the naked eye, you will eventually need binoculars to identify birds farther away. Binoculars are described according to their power (the degree to which they appear to magnify a distant object, for instance 8x or 10x) and the diameter of the distant (objective) lens, in millimeters. The best binoculars for birding are 7x35, 8x40, 10x40, or some similar configuration. Binoculars more powerful than 10x are difficult to hold steady. Binoculars with larger objective lenses (greater than 35mm) admit more light and are easier to use in many situations, but they are also heavier than a compact model. Be sure to find a pair that focuses with one central knob and that allows you to focus on objects that are close to you (preferably within 15 feet). And buy the best you can afford. Looking through poor-quality optics for hours at a time can be tiring and frustrating.

For observing waterfowl and shorebirds at great distances, you might want to purchase a spotting telescope, as well. Good scopes are expensive but are indispensable in certain birding situations. Most have interchangeable or zoom eyepieces ranging in power from 15x to 60x; 20x to 30x is the most useful range. A sturdy tripod is a must for steadying a scope and protecting it from being blown over.

Finding Birds. Birds are everywhere. Once you start looking, you will wonder how you could previously have been so unaware of their presence, and you will be astounded by the remarkable number of species that can be found even in a city park or suburban garden.

Although many familiar and widespread birds can be found in a variety of habitats (which is why we think of them as common), most species are adapted to a particular environment. This is the key to finding birds and is crucial in learning how to identify them.

For example, American Robins, which are common in city parks and backyards, also nest in rural woodlots bordering farms and upland pastures. Breeding in those same pastures and hayfields, however, is a community of bird species, including Bobolinks, Meadowlarks, and Savannah and Grasshopper Sparrows—none of which would ever turn up in a suburban backyard. If you wanted to find any of these open-country birds, you would first need to locate the right habitat.

Some habitats evolve over time, attracting a distinct community of birds during each phase. Abandoned farm fields and cleared forest will eventually revert to woodland if left alone; this process is known as *succession.* The fields first become "weedy" and overgrown with grasses and wildflowers. As tree saplings and shrubs become established, the field can then be described as "brushy." With additional time, as the young trees shade out grasses and herbs, the habitat is known as "second growth." Finally, when the canopy of trees has grown taller and the shady understory becomes more open, the old field is considered a woodland.

Another crucial consideration in bird finding is the time of year. Soon after you begin birdwatching, you will notice that some of the birds in your backyard come and go with the seasons. Chickadees and jays are resident year round, while orioles are common only in summer, and juncos visit during winter months. Others, such as warblers, may be present for just a month in spring or fall. If you were to return in midwinter to the same rural hayfields described earlier, few of those nesting species would still be there. Instead you would find Horned Larks, Snow Buntings, and possibly a Rough-legged Hawk.

Gradually, the association of certain birds with their preferred habitats will become second nature to you. When you flush a sparrow from the ground, you will be able to eliminate most possibilities simply by considering where you are and what season it is.

When looking for birds, don't forget that they are often most active early and late in the day. This is especially true of male songbirds during nesting season. They greet each day with a song to attract a mate or to reestablish their territories. However, they usually become quiet by midmorning. Small birds are easily missed in the lush summer foliage, which is why their vocalizations can be so helpful in alerting you to their presence and helping you identify them. If you have ever accompanied an experienced birder, you will surely have been impressed by the many species he or she identified by voice alone.

Looking at Birds. Bird identification is a process of elimination. When you spot a new bird, try first to place it into the broadest of categories, using as points of reference those basic avian images we all learn as children. For instance, does it swim like a duck? Does it soar like a hawk or a gull? Does it look like a pigeon or a jay or a sparrow?

If the bird is entirely unfamiliar, ask yourself the following series of questions: What is it doing? How big is it? What is its shape? How are its beak, legs, and wings shaped? What color is it? Does it have any noticeable markings? Then, using the Master Plates in this book as a guide, try to place the bird into its family group. At first you will be stumped by many of the new birds you find. Don't feel compelled to name every sparrow lurking in the brush. Be satisfied just figuring out that it actually is a sparrow and not a wren or a warbler! And remember that seasoned birders, whose snap identifications may intimidate you, are usually drawing upon years of experience.

Behavior. What a bird is doing can often reveal its family affiliation. Although it may seem foolishly obvious, ducks swim, woodpeckers climb tree trunks, and hummingbirds hover. Other behavioral clues may be more subtle. The familiar Mallard and other freshwater ducks feed by dabbling in shallow water, while diving and sea ducks submerge entirely, swimming underwater for minutes at a time. Similarly, most terns plunge headfirst into the surf, while the closely related gulls pluck food from the surface of the water. Posture is also very important. Flycatchers sit upright, while other small greenish birds, such as vireos, warblers, and kinglets, perch horizontally. Behavioral twitches or habits may also help confirm an identification. Wrens characteristically cock their tails up over their backs. Spotted Sandpipers bob and teeter as they walk. Eastern Phoebes wave their tails emphatically. And the Hermit Thrush can be distinguished from other spotted thrushes—even in the dark, dappled shadows of the forest undergrowth—by its habit of slowly pumping its tail.

Size. Noticing whether a bird is huge or particularly tiny is easy. But how about all of those in between? In the field, try to estimate a bird's size relative to a more familiar species. Is it smaller than a spar-

PARTS OF A BIRD

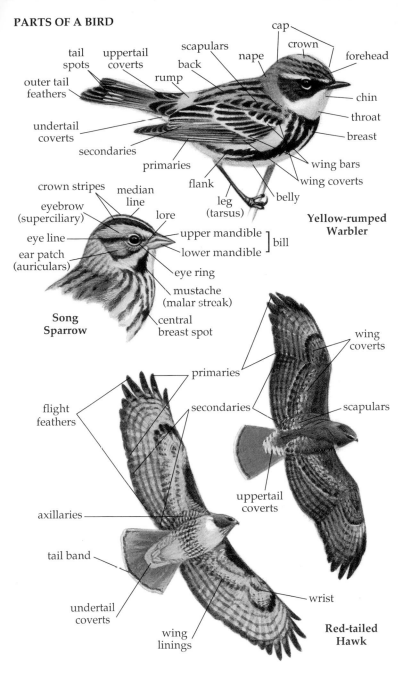

cap
crown
forehead
scapulars
nape
back
tail spots
uppertail coverts
rump
outer tail feathers
chin
throat
breast
undertail coverts
secondaries
primaries
flank
wing bars
wing coverts
leg (tarsus)
belly

Yellow-rumped Warbler

crown stripes
median line
eyebrow (superciliary)
lore
eye line
upper mandible
lower mandible
} bill
ear patch (auriculars)
eye ring
mustache (malar streak)
central breast spot

Song Sparrow

primaries
wing coverts
secondaries
scapulars
flight feathers
uppertail coverts
axillaries
tail band
wrist
undertail coverts
wing linings

Red-tailed Hawk

row? Robin-sized? Crow-sized? About the size of a Mallard? In some situations, you might be able to compare an unidentified bird with a known bird in the same field of view. Even experts use this method to help them separate look-alikes such as the Greater and Lesser Yellowlegs.

Measurements given in this guide are average lengths, from the tip of the bill to the end of the tail. They are provided for comparative purposes.

Shape. There is no single characteristic more crucial to bird identification than shape. Color and plumage can vary with the sex and age of a bird, and with the time of year—but shape is structural. Each individual of a particular species shares the same basic shape.

Consider first a bird's overall proportions when trying to determine its family affiliation. Is it squat, like a pigeon, or tall and slender, like an egret? Is its neck short and thick, like an owl's, or elongated, like an ibis's? Is its head relatively small and round, like a pigeon's, or angular and oversized, like a kingfisher's? How are its wings shaped? Long and slender, like a tern's? Short and rounded, like a quail's? And are the wing tips pointed, like the tern's? Or are the outer feathers *(primaries)* spread into "fingers," as on a soaring crow or Red-tailed Hawk?

Note also the bird's legs. Wading birds, such as herons, ibis, and many shorebirds, have tall, spindly legs and slender toes. But water birds that spend most of their time in the air, such as terns, have short, stubby legs with webbed toes.

What shape is the beak? Herons, terns, and kingfishers, all fish eaters, have sharp, daggerlike beaks. Ibis have long, down-curved, probing bills. Other waders and shorebirds have a variety of slender beaks. Flesh-eating hawks and owls have sharp, hooked beaks. On smaller songbirds the shape of the beak varies between two extremes: a thick, conical beak for cracking seeds, as on finches and grosbeaks; and a thin, sharp beak for eating insects, as on wrens, warblers, and kinglets. Keep in mind that as your skills improve, you will learn to see the subtle distinctions that separate similar species. You will notice, for instance, that wrens' slender beaks, when compared with those of kinglets or warblers, have a unique, slightly down-curved shape. Birds that all looked alike when you started birdwatching will take on their own distinctive forms.

Field Marks. Any color, plumage pattern, or marking that is unique to a particular species or group of birds (and is therefore useful for identification) is considered a *field mark*. Memorizing all the intricate markings and patterns of hundreds of birds would take years of experience. The key to using field marks is understanding the range of possible markings and where on a bird they can be found. Start by studying the illustrations defining the parts of a bird.

Plumages. All birds lose their feathers and grow replacements, or *molt*, at regular intervals (once or twice a year for most songbirds; once every 3 to 4 years for large raptors, such as eagles). During its lifetime a bird may "molt through" several distinct plumages. But keep in mind that each individual of a species may be in a slightly different stage of molt on a given day, or may be in some intermediate plumage not shown in any book.

Here are some common terms used in *Eastern Birds* to describe the plumages of birds:

Male, female. Although in some species the sexes look alike, many birds have different plumages for male and female; that is, they are *sexually dimorphic.*

Breeding, nonbreeding. Most species molt into a breeding plumage in late winter and early spring, prior to the nesting season. Males, in particular, often acquire showy and colorful breeding plumages. Nonbreeding plumage is acquired after breeding, usually in mid to late summer, and is retained through the winter.

Summer, winter, spring, fall. These seasonal labels are often more meaningful to the casual birder than *breeding* and *nonbreeding* and thus are frequently used in *Eastern Birds*. However, to avoid confusion, *breeding* and *nonbreeding* have been used when referring to species that nest in the far north and winter in Central and South America, passing through our area only during spring and fall migrations. Of the more than 30 species of wood-warblers, for example, many are seen in their flashy "summer" plumages only during spring migration, which is completed by early June. Similarly, many types of shorebirds are seen only during their southward migration in mid to late summer—after they have molted into their drab "winter" plumages.

Adult, juvenile, immature, subadult. These terms refer to distinctive age groups. Unless otherwise noted, the birds illustrated in *Eastern Birds* are adults. Juveniles are fledglings in their first true plumage. This "juvenal" plumage is usually retained for just a brief period and is seldom seen by birders. However, in some cases—for example, Yellow-bellied Sapsuckers and numerous shorebirds—juveniles are seen well into their first winter. Most juvenile songbirds molt into an immature plumage prior to leaving the breeding ground, and remain immatures until they molt into adult plumage the following spring. Many larger birds, such as gulls and hawks, do not become mature for up to 3 or 4 years and, following their juvenal plumage, molt through a series of identifiable immature plumages (*first-winter, second-winter,* etc.), the last of which may also be known as *subadult.*

Subspecies. Widely distributed species with far-flung or isolated populations are often subdivided by ornithologists into *subspecies* (also known as "races"). Subspecies with distinctive plumages that might be confusing to a birder have been illustrated whenever possible.

Morph. Individuals within some species may occur in differently colored plumages, called *morphs* (also called "phases"). By definition, the occurrence of morphs in a population of birds is independent of subspecies, gender, age, or time of year.

SWIMMING BIRDS
OF SALTWATER BAYS AND THE OCEAN
(all shown in winter plumages)

Herring Gull, first-winter, p. 74

Brant, p. 32

Oldsquaw, female, p. 42

Black Guillemot, p. 28

Double-crested Cormorant, immature, p. 30

Common Loon, p. 26

Bonaparte's Gull, immature, p. 76

Horned Grebe, p. 26

SWIMMING BIRDS
OF PONDS, LAKES, AND MARSHES
(all shown in summer plumages)

Ring-necked Duck, female, p. 38

Ruddy Duck, p. 38
female   male

Hooded Merganser, female, p. 40

American Wigeon, female, p. 36

Eared Grebe, p. 26

Wood Duck, female, p. 36

Green-winged Teal, female, p. 36

Gadwall, male, p. 34

12

adult male

Common Eider, p. 42

immature males

female

Surf Scoter, p. 42

male

female

Red-breasted Merganser, p. 40

male

male

Common Goldeneye, p. 40

female

male

Greater Scaup, p. 38

Bufflehead, female, p. 40

Canada Goose, p. 32

American White Pelican, p. 30

Tundra Swan, p. 32

Snow Goose, p. 32

Franklin's Gull, p. 76

Pied-billed Grebe, p. 26

American Coot, p. 62

Wilson's Phalarope, p. 70

13

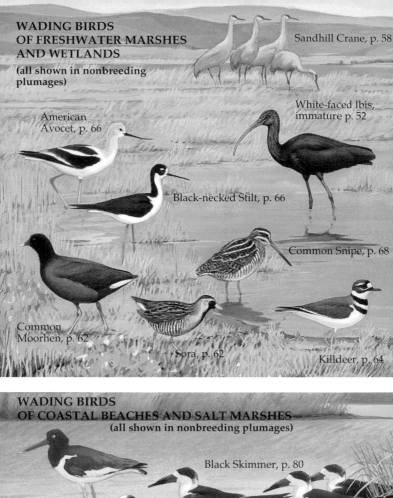

WADING BIRDS
OF FRESHWATER MARSHES
AND WETLANDS

(all shown in nonbreeding plumages)

Sandhill Crane, p. 58

American Avocet, p. 66

White-faced Ibis, immature p. 52

Black-necked Stilt, p. 66

Common Snipe, p. 68

Common Moorhen, p. 62

Sora, p. 62

Killdeer, p. 64

WADING BIRDS
OF COASTAL BEACHES AND SALT MARSHES

(all shown in nonbreeding plumages)

Black Skimmer, p. 80

American Oystercatcher, p. 66

Common Tern, p. 78

Willet, p. 70

Sanderling, p. 72

Short-billed Dowitcher, p. 68

Ruddy Turnstone, p. 64

14

Double-crested Cormorant, immature, p. 30

Great Blue Heron, p. 58

Black-crowned Night-Heron, immature, p. 54

Snowy Egret, p. 56

Lesser Yellowlegs, p. 70

Spotted Sandpiper, p. 70

Green Heron, immature, p. 54

Clapper Rail, p. 62

Whimbrel, p. 66

Laughing Gull, juvenile, p. 76

Black-bellied Plover, p. 64

Semipalmated Plover, p. 64

Dunlin, p. 72

15

LARGER BIRDS IN FLIGHT
"HAWK-LIKE" BIRDS

Turkey Vulture, p. 44

Great Blue
Heron, p. 58

Bald Eagle,
immature,
p. 44

American
Crow,
p. 104

Red-tailed Hawk,
immature, p. 48

Cooper's
Hawk,
immature,
p. 50

Short-eared
Owl, p. 88

Peregrine
Falcon,
immature,
p. 50

Rough-legged
Hawk, light morph,
immature, p. 48

Northern
Harrier,
female,
p. 46

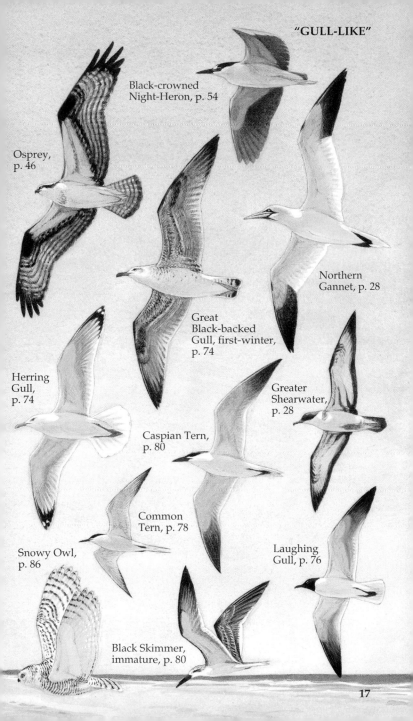

Black-crowned
Night-Heron, p. 54

Osprey,
p. 46

Northern
Gannet, p. 28

Great
Black-backed
Gull, first-winter,
p. 74

Herring
Gull,
p. 74

Greater
Shearwater,
p. 28

Caspian Tern,
p. 80

Common
Tern, p. 78

Snowy Owl,
p. 86

Laughing
Gull, p. 76

Black Skimmer,
immature, p. 80

COMMON ROADSIDE BIRDS

European Starling, p.136

Tree Swallow and Barn Swallows, p. 102

Belted Kingfisher, male, p. 92

Northern Flicker, male, p. 94

Red-tailed Hawk, p. 48

Mourning Dove, p. 82

Eastern Bluebird, male, p. 116

American Robin, p. 116

Scissor-tailed Flycatcher, p. 98

Northern Bobwhite, p. 60

American Crow, p. 104

Common Nighthawk, p. 90

male

American Kestrel, p. 50

female

Red-headed Woodpecker, p. 94

European Starling, p. 136

Eastern Kingbird, p. 98

Common Grackle, p. 136

Red-winged Blackbird, male, p. 134

Eastern Meadowlark, p. 134

Red-winged Blackbird, male, p. 134

Killdeer, p. 64

American Goldfinch, male, p. 150

Northern Flicker, female, p. 94

Horned Lark, p. 148

19

Tufted Titmouse, p. 106

COMMON BACKYARD BIRDS

Blue Jay, p. 104

Black-capped Chickadee, p. 106

Cedar Waxwing, p. 116

White-breasted Nuthatch, p. 108

Brown Creeper, p. 108

American Goldfinch, winter male, p. 150

Evening Grosbeak, female, p. 152

Downy Woodpecker, male, p. 96

House Finch, male, p. 150

Mourning Dove, p. 82

White-throated Sparrow, p. 144

Dark-eyed Junco, p. 142

Northern Cardinal, female, p. 140

House Sparrow, male, p. 152

Carolina Wren, p. 110

Chimney Swift, p. 90

Rose-breasted Grosbeak, breeding male p. 140

Northern Oriole, male, p. 138

Northern Mockingbird, p. 112

Wood Thrush, p. 114

Rufous-sided Towhee, male, p. 142

American Robin, p. 116

Brown Thrasher, p. 112

Common Grackle, p. 136

European Starling, p. 136

adult

juvenile

Chipping Sparrow, p. 142

Song Sparrow, p. 144

Ruby-throated Hummingbird, male, p. 92

Gray Catbird, p. 112

Common Yellowthroat, male, p. 124

21

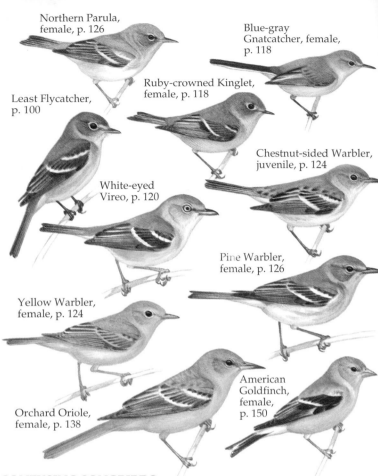

Northern Parula, female, p. 126

Blue-gray Gnatcatcher, female, p. 118

Ruby-crowned Kinglet, female, p. 118

Least Flycatcher, p. 100

Chestnut-sided Warbler, juvenile, p. 124

White-eyed Vireo, p. 120

Pine Warbler, female, p. 126

Yellow Warbler, female, p. 124

American Goldfinch, female, p. 150

Orchard Oriole, female, p. 138

CONFUSING SONGBIRDS
grayish to greenish with eye ring and/or wing bars

Northern Parula—small; yellow throat; pointed, bicolored bill.

Blue-gray Gnatcatcher—small, slender; long tail; thin bill; active.

Least Flycatcher— wide bill; upright posture; flycatching behavior.

Ruby-crowned Kinglet—small and compact; thin bill; very active.

White-eyed Vireo—chunky shape; stout bill; yellow "spectacles."

Chestnut-sided Warbler—white eye ring; gray face; yellow wing bars.

Pine Warbler—variable plumage; long tail; largish bill; pinewoods.

Yellow Warbler—yellow-green; yellow tail spots; beady black eye.

Orchard Oriole—larger than warbler; greenish above; pointed bill.

American Goldfinch—pink, conical bill; white rump; notched tail.

House Wren, p. 110

Eastern Phoebe, p. 100

Warbling Vireo, p. 118

Common Yellowthroat, immature female, p. 124

Black-throated Blue Warbler, female, p. 128

Orange-crowned Warbler, p. 132

Painted Bunting, female, p. 140

Scarlet Tanager, female, p. 138

CONFUSING SONGBIRDS

Brownish to greenish; drab, without conspicuous markings

House Wren—hunched posture; short, cocked tail; thin, curved bill.

Eastern Phoebe—dark head; upright flycatcher posture; wags tail.

Common Yellowthroat—yellow throat; dingy underparts; low thickets.

Warbling Vireo—thick bill; pale eyebrow; sluggish; in shade trees.

Black-throated Blue Warbler—narrow white eyebrow; white wing spot.

Orange-crowned Warbler—pale yellow undertail coverts; blurry breast streaks; pointy bill.

Painted Bunting—thick, finch bill; bright apple-green upperparts.

Scarlet Tanager—thick bill; dusky wings and tail; chunky; sluggish.

Rose-breasted Grosbeak, female, p. 140

Pine Siskin, p. 150

Purple Finch, female, p. 150

House Finch, female, p. 150

Song Sparrow, p. 144

Chipping Sparrow, winter, p. 142

Dickcissel, female, p. 146

Indigo Bunting, female, p. 140

House Sparrow, female, p. 152

Brown-headed Cowbird, female, p. 136

Blue Grosbeak, female, p. 140

CONFUSING SONGBIRDS
brownish, "finchlike"

Pine Siskin—small; sharp, pointed bill; yellow in tail and wings.

Rose-breasted Grosbeak—large size; pale, massive beak; *eek* call.

Purple Finch—stocky; notched tail; conical bill; dark malar patches.

House Finch—slender build; conical bill; densely streaked overall.

Song Sparrow—long, rounded tail; dark malar streaks; breast spot.

Chipping Sparrow—small, slender; dark eye line; streaked brownish crown.

House Sparrow—dingy gray underparts; buff eyebrow; yellowish bill.

Dickcissel—yellow on breast and eyebrow; fine malar streak; gray bill; Great Plains.

Indigo Bunting—small size; warm brown plumage; faint breast streaks.

Blue Grosbeak—warm brown plumage; cinnamon wing bars; large bill.

Brown-headed Cowbird—gray-brown; faintly streaked below; conical bill.

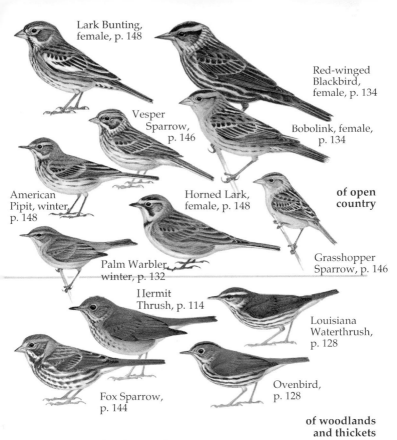

Lark Bunting, female, p. 148

Red-winged Blackbird, female, p. 134

Vesper Sparrow, p. 146

Bobolink, female, p. 134

American Pipit, winter, p. 148

Horned Lark, female, p. 148

of open country

Palm Warbler, winter, p. 132

Grasshopper Sparrow, p. 146

Hermit Thrush, p. 114

Louisiana Waterthrush, p. 128

Fox Sparrow, p. 144

Ovenbird, p. 128

of woodlands and thickets

CONFUSING SONGBIRDS
brownish, streaky

Lark Bunting—stocky; stout grayish beak; white in wing; Great Plains.

Red-winged Blackbird—dark; heavily streaked plumage; tapered, sharp, conical bill; buff face.

Bobolink—buffy plumage; boldly striped back; finchlike bill.

Grasshopper Sparrow—small; short tail; unstreaked buff breast.

Vesper Sparrow—finely streaked breast; white outer tail feathers.

American Pipit—slender; thin bill; white outer tail feathers; terrestrial; pumps tail.

Horned Lark—squat posture; dark chest mark and face pattern; black tail edged white; terrestrial.

Palm Warbler—small; thin bill; yellow undertail coverts; wags tail.

Hermit Thrush—olive back, rusty tail; spotted breast; thin bill.

Fox Sparrow—back streaked gray and rust; bright rusty tail; conical bill.

Louisiana Waterthrush—dark brown back; white eyebrow; bobbing gait; near water.

Ovenbird—unstreaked olive back; black-bordered orange crown; bold eye ring.

LOONS A family of diving water birds with sharp, daggerlike beaks. Their powerful webbed feet are so far back on their bodies that the birds can barely maneuver on land. Loons nest along northern lake shores and winter along seacoasts and on saltwater bays and the Great Lakes. In breeding plumage they are easy to distinguish, but winter-plumage birds present a greater challenge. From a distance, loons may be confused with mergansers, which are sleeker; cormorants, which have longer necks and tails; or grebes, which are smaller and more compact.

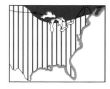

COMMON LOON *Gavia immer.* 31½" (80 cm). Larger than a duck, with a thick neck and stout, straight bill. Unmistakable in summer; in winter the neck collar, though faint, can often still be seen. This is our only loon likely to be seen in breeding plumage. Its eerie yodel-like call is a familiar summer sound of the northern lake country. The smaller, paler **Red-throated Loon** winters within the same range (except on the Gulf Coast); its profile, with a flatter crown and thinner, upturned bill, is distinctive.

GREBES Another strictly aquatic family of adept swimmers and divers. Superficially ducklike, grebes are told by their longer, thinner necks; narrow, pointed bills; and lack of discernible tails. Their toes are lobed rather than webbed. Grebes build their nests on floating mounds of vegetation in freshwater ponds and marshes. Hatchlings of most species are boldly striped and get about by riding piggyback on their parents.

HORNED GREBE *Podiceps auritus.* 13½" (35 cm). Breeding bird unmistakable; in winter, look for white cheeks, throat, and neck, offset by dark cap and line down back of neck. Nests on prairie ponds and marshes. Common during migration and in winter along the coast. The **Red-necked Grebe**, which also winters offshore, is larger, with a long, dusky neck and heavier bill.

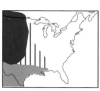

EARED GREBE *Podiceps nigricollis.* 13" (33 cm). Breeding adult unmistakable; in winter very similar to Horned Grebe, but note slightly upturned bill, steeply peaked forehead, and dusky face pattern. Primarily a Western species, but nests on lakes and marshes of the prairie states.

PIED-BILLED GREBE *Podilymbus podiceps.* 13½" (35 cm). Note lollipop head shape and pale chickenlike bill with black ring (lacking in winter). Our most common and widespread grebe, the Pied-billed prefers freshwater habitats year-round. Often swims with only its head visible.

LOONS AND GREBES

Common

Red-throated

Horned Grebe
(to show scale)

Winter-Plumage Loons

COMMON LOON   summer

HORNED
GREBE

summer

winter

EARED
GREBE

winter

summer (on nest)

chicks riding
piggyback

summer

PIED-BILLED
GREBE

partially
submerged

winter

MISCELLANEOUS SEABIRDS The following members of four strictly oceanic bird families are the only true seabirds likely to be encountered by a beginner. They may be seen in season from a boat just offshore and occasionally even from land using powerful binoculars or a spotting scope. To appreciate the full diversity and richness of birdlife out at sea, however, refer to a more comprehensive guide (p. 157).

NORTHERN GANNET *Sula bassanus*. 37" (95 cm). Wingspan 6' (1.75 m). Huge; adults white with extensive black wing tips; immatures variably dark above, acquiring adult plumage over 3 years. At any age the hefty pointed beak, wedge-shaped tail, and long, narrow wings give gannets a unique shape. Look for them out beyond the surf, diving from great heights headfirst into the water. Even from far away, adults appear conspicuously white. Note that even the largest terns are much smaller and that gulls do not dive.

GREATER SHEARWATER *Puffinis gravis*. 19½" (50 cm). Gull-sized. Shearwaters are identifiable by their flight, which alternates between several quick flaps and a glide on stiff outstretched wings often just above the waves. The wings may appear to "shear" the water's surface. The Greater is told by its two-toned appearance and dark cap. The **Sooty Shearwater**, a fairly common summer visitor to our offshore waters, is dusky gray with whitish wing linings. Look for shearwaters among flocks of gulls following fishing boats.

WILSON'S STORM-PETREL *Oceanites oceanicus*. 7" (18 cm). Small (starling-sized) and seemingly hyperactive, Wilson's Storm-petrels glide and flutter low over the water. This is by far our most abundant storm-petrel species, often seen in great numbers during the summer, feeding in ships' wakes, with long, slender legs dangling beneath them, feet tapping the surface. They nest on islands in the Antarctic during winter.

BLACK GUILLEMOT *Cepphus grylle*. 13" (33 cm). Pigeon-sized; unmistakable in summer, rarely seen in winter. Along the coasts of Maine and Canada's Maritimes, this is the only member of the alcid family likely to be seen from shore. Alcids are the Northern Hemisphere's equivalent of penguins: mostly black and white, compact swimmers and divers that, although able to fly, are more agile swimming underwater. They nest in huge mixed colonies on cliffs and rocky islands of the northern oceans; most winter far offshore.

MISCELLANEOUS SEABIRDS

NORTHERN GANNET

adult

third-year immature

first-year immature

diving

first-winter Herring Gull for comparison

GREATER SHEARWATER

WILSON'S STORM-PETREL

BLACK GUILLEMOT

summer

winter

CORMORANTS AND ANHINGAS These closely related families of fish-eating water birds often perch with their wings spread to dry. Cormorants are mostly black in color, with heavy bodies, long necks, and long, hooked beaks. At home in salt or fresh water, they swim low in the water, heads tilted upward, and dive for prey from the surface. Flocks often fly in loose formation. Anhingas are slimmer, with longer tails, serpentine necks, and thin, spearlike bills. Only one species lives in North America.

DOUBLE-CRESTED CORMORANT *Phalacrocorax auritus*. 31" (80 cm). Adult black with an unfeathered orange throat pouch; breeding plumage "crests" hard to see. Immature dingy brown, paler on the neck and breast. Our most common and widespread cormorant and the only species likely to be seen inland. The larger **Great Cormorant** winters along the Atlantic coast (rare south of New Jersey). Look for the adult's white-bordered throat pouch. Young Great Cormorant is brownish with a white belly. A third species, the smaller **Neotropic Cormorant**, is a fairly common resident along the western Gulf Coast.

ANHINGA *Anhinga anhinga*. 34½" (89 cm). Slender and lanky, with an ample tail and white streaks on back plumes and wing coverts. Resident of southeastern rivers, swamps, and mangroves, the Anhinga often swims submerged with only its head and neck visible.

PELICANS Familiar large water birds having huge beaks and expandable throat pouches. These sacs are not used for storage, as popular culture has it, but as fishing nets. Most species fish as they swim, sweeping their beaks through surface waters. Brown Pelicans use spectacular plunging dives to snatch deeper-swimming prey.

BROWN PELICAN *Pelecanus occidentalis*. 48" (123 cm). Wingspan 7' (2.1 m). Adults unmistakable. Immature birds uniformly dull brown. Small flocks fly in formation low over the surf, then rise with unexpected grace as each bird prepares to dive, in turn, into the waves below. Strictly coastal from Texas north to Virginia and, rarely, to New Jersey. Range has been expanding in recent years.

AMERICAN WHITE PELICAN *Pelecanus erythrorhynchos*. 61" (156 cm). Wingspan exceeds 9' (2.7 m). Immense and unmistakable. Often soars at great heights; note that the Wood Stork, comparable in size and plumage, flies with neck extended and long legs trailing. Nesting colonies, found on prairie-lake islands, are now scarce.

CORMORANTS, ANHINGAS, AND PELICANS

Double-crested

GREAT CORMORANT

adult

female

immature

male

adult

DOUBLE-CRESTED CORMORANT

ANHINGA

female Anhinga swimming

breeding

immature

Brown

White

BROWN PELICAN

AMERICAN WHITE PELICAN

nonbreeding

WATERFOWL Swans, geese, and ducks make up this family of web-footed water birds. Waterfowl beaks vary from the classic spatula-shaped bills of dabbling ducks to the narrow, serrated, fish-grasping bills of mergansers and the stubby grazing bills of geese. Subgroups are further distinguished by shape, feeding behavior, and nesting habits. The longer necks of swans and geese let them reach deeper aquatic vegetation from the surface without diving. Geese also graze on land.

TUNDRA SWAN *Cygnus columbianus*. 52½" (134 cm). Formerly known as Whistling Swan. Large and white; black bill with variable yellow spot at base. In the East this is our only native swan; the more familiar **Mute Swan**, found in parks, on protected coastal bays, and, locally, on the Great Lakes, was introduced from Europe. Mute Swans are told by their gracefully curved necks and orange bills with protruding black knob.

SNOW GOOSE *Chen caerulescens*. 28½" (74 cm). Variable species; occurs in two color morphs, as shown, as well as intermediate "hybrids." Extent of rusty stains on the head and neck may also vary. Immature "blue" morph (not shown) is overall dusky gray, paler on the wings. Snow Geese migrate in huge flocks from their Arctic nesting grounds to the mid-Atlantic and Gulf Coast segments of their winter range. The blue morph is rare on the East Coast but rather common along the Gulf Coast.

GREATER WHITE-FRONTED GOOSE *Anser albifrons*. 29" (74 cm). Grayish-brown with pale belly and white undertail; note pink bill with white around base (lacking on immatures) and dark blotches on belly. Often seen among flocks of other geese feeding on grainfields and on marshes. Rare east of the Mississippi.

CANADA GOOSE *Branta canadensis*. 24" (62 cm) to 44" (111 cm). Pale breast, black head and neck, and white face patch make this species easy to identify. Our largest, longest-necked goose, this familiar and increasingly widespread species nests in city parks and on golf courses, marshes, and ponds.

BRANT *Branta bernicla*. 24½" (63 cm). Small and compact; bold pattern of blackish foreparts with pale belly and white undertail coverts is evident even from a distance; note small pale markings on sides of neck. A coastal species; fairly common in winter on bays and salt marshes, and along shores from Maine to the Carolinas; rare inland. Breeds in the Arctic.

immature

adult

Mute Swan

Tundra Swan

"Blue"

Snow

White-fronted

TUNDRA SWAN

white morph
immature

SNOW
GOOSE

adult

GREATER
WHITE-FRONTED
GOOSE

blue
morph

Brant

Canada

CANADA
GOOSE

BRANT

SWANS AND GEESE

DABBLING DUCKS These are surface-feeding ducks, found primarily on fresh and brackish water. Most tip forward, with rear ends pointing up, as they feed on submerged plants, seeds, and invertebrates. Males usually have bold, distinctive plumages; the mottled, brownish females mostly look alike and are harder to identify. With practice, they can be recognized by their size and characteristic shape, and by the color and pattern of their wing patches. Most species have a conspicuous patch of feathers, called the *speculum*, on the trailing edge of the wing. During summer, males molt briefly into dull, femalelike garb, called the *eclipse plumage*. They are flightless while in eclipse.

MALLARD *Anas platyrhynchos*. 23" (51 cm). Breeding male is unmistakable. Female larger than most comparable ducks; note orange bill with dusky markings, white outer tail feathers, and shiny blue speculum bordered with white. This is the familiar duck of city parks, marinas, ponds, and marshes. It is the ancestor of most domestic ducks. Its nest is hidden amid dense, grassy vegetation, sometimes far from water.

AMERICAN BLACK DUCK *Anas rubripes*. 23" (51 cm). Sexes look alike, resembling female Mallard but with body much darker brown; bill is greenish-yellow (female's has dusky markings). In flight, white wing linings are flashier than on other ducks. Common but declining on northeastern coastal salt marshes, wetlands, and inland ponds. Black Ducks sometimes interbreed with Mallards, producing hybrids with mixed traits. The **Mottled Duck**, a resident of Florida and the Gulf Coast, is slightly lighter brown than the Black Duck. The sexes look alike.

NORTHERN PINTAIL *Anas acuta*. Male 27" (69 cm), female 21½" (55 cm). Male's pin tail and bold head and neck pattern are diagnostic. Female slimmer than hen Mallard, with a longer neck, all-dark pointed tail, and grayish bill; also lacks Mallard's blue speculum. A common nesting species in midwestern prairie potholes, less common in the eastern portion of their range.

GADWALL *Anas strepera*. 20" (52 cm). Male grayish with black around tail and a dark gray bill. Female resembles female Mallard, but look for her white belly and darker tail. In both sexes, the small white speculum (obvious in flight) may be visible on the sides of swimming birds. Fairly common on freshwater ponds and marshes, but inconspicuous and easily overlooked.

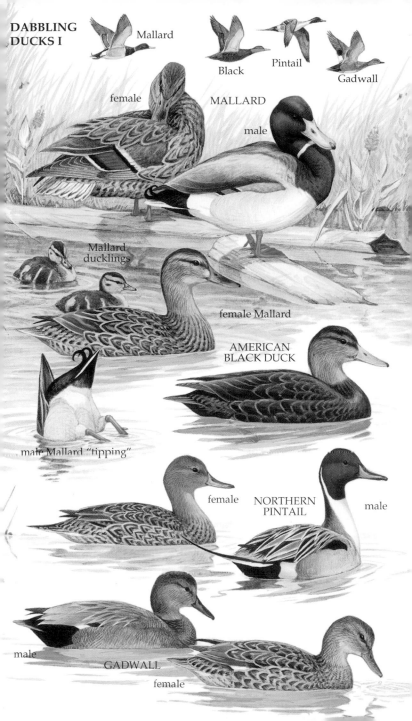

DABBLING DUCKS I

Mallard

Black

Pintail

Gadwall

female

MALLARD

male

Mallard ducklings

female Mallard

AMERICAN BLACK DUCK

male Mallard "tipping"

female

NORTHERN PINTAIL

male

male

GADWALL

female

AMERICAN WIGEON *Anas americana*. 20" (51 cm). Male has conspicuous white forehead and patches on flank. Female is rusty-brown, grayer on the head, with a dark smudge around the eye. Note the dark-tipped, bluish bill. Also look for the green speculum and the broad white patch on the forewing of flying Wigeon. The male **Eurasian Wigeon**, a rare winter visitor, has a gray body, russet head, and yellowish crown (female closely resembles the female American Wigeon). Wigeon nest in various freshwater habitats; in winter they often flock with scaup and other diving ducks on coastal bays, marshes, and inlets.

GREEN-WINGED TEAL *Anas crecca*. 14½" (37 cm). Our smallest dabbling duck. Male has a reddish-brown head with a green patch. Female looks like a tiny female Mallard, with a dark bill and a green speculum; unlike female Blue-winged Teal, she lacks wing patches. This common and widespread duck nests on freshwater ponds and marshes. In winter it also inhabits saltwater marshes or inlets.

BLUE-WINGED TEAL *Anas discors*. 15½" (40 cm). Male is our only dabbling duck with a white crescent-shaped mark on the face. The female resembles a small, dark-billed female Mallard, but note her large sky-blue wing patches and green speculum. Common breeder on prairie ponds of the Midwest and Great Plains; less common elsewhere within its range.

NORTHERN SHOVELER *Anas clypeata*. 19" (49 cm). Shovelers swim with their large, shovel-shaped bills pointed downward, and when feeding, skim the surface, sifting water and silt through their beaks. Male's plumage suggests Mallard's, but chestnut is on the sides rather than on the breast. Also note the large sky-blue wing patches. Female similar to hen Mallard but distinguished by her bill shape and teal-like wing pattern. Fairly common and widespread.

WOOD DUCK *Aix sponsa*. 18½" (47 cm). Male is unmistakable. Female is best told by her overall shape, broad white eye ring, and white throat. Wood Ducks have longish tails, particularly evident in flight. They inhabit wooded swamps and ponds and nest in tree cavities, often high above the ground. After hatching, the chicks climb out and leap to the ground, apparently without harm. Wood Ducks readily accept large nest boxes set up in a suitable habitat.

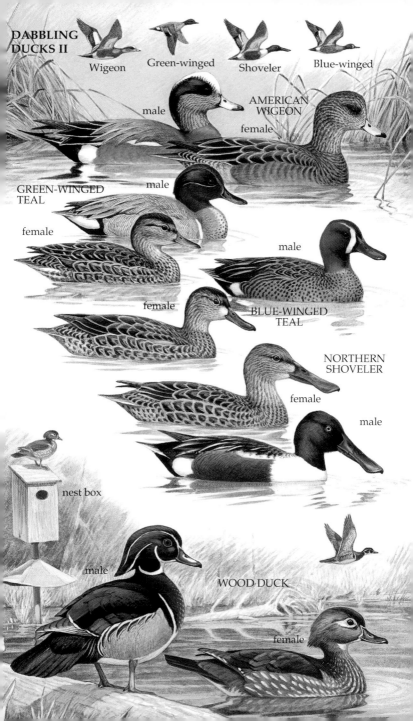

DABBLING
DUCKS II

Wigeon   Green-winged   Shoveler   Blue-winged

male

AMERICAN
WIGEON

female

GREEN-WINGED
TEAL

male

female

male

female   BLUE-WINGED
TEAL

NORTHERN
SHOVELER

female

male

nest box

male

WOOD DUCK

female

DIVING DUCKS As their name implies, these ducks dive underwater to feed on fish, invertebrates, and seaweed. They include the bay ducks (or pochards) and stiff-tailed ducks shown on this page, and the goldeneyes, mergansers, scoters, and eiders shown on pp. 40 to 43. Diving ducks have squat legs set far back on their bodies; they can barely waddle and do not graze on land. In winter large flocks (called *rafts*) gather on lakes, rivers, coastal marshes, bays, and ocean, where they may mingle with loons, grebes, coots, and other waterfowl. Recently many species have become scarce due to overhunting and development of the prairie wetlands on which they nest.

CANVASBACK *Aythya valisineria*. 21" (54 cm). Note the unique sloping forehead and long bill. Male's unmarked white back and sides are noticeable from a distance. Female is distinguished from other bay ducks by her distinctive head shape and pale gray body.

REDHEAD *Aythya americana*. 19½" (50 cm). Male has steel-gray body, black chest, and reddish head. Female is paler brown than female scaup, with a more diffuse pale area around her beak; told from Canvasback and Ring-necked by her rounder head. Fairly common breeding duck of prairie marshes; uncommon on the East Coast.

LESSER SCAUP *Aythya affinis*. 16½" (42.5 cm). Male has glossy blackish head, white sides, and pale grayish back. Female is dark brown with sharply defined white patch around base of bill. The **Greater Scaup** is nearly identical; look for its rounder head, larger bill, and more extensive white wing stripe. In winter the Greater is the common scaup of the Northeast coast and Great Lakes; the Lesser predominates inland and on fresh water and is especially common in the South.

RING-NECKED DUCK *Aythya collaris*. 16½" (42.5 cm). Male is our only black-backed "bay" duck; also note peaked crown and white mark on sides of breast. Female has angular head shape and thin white eye ring. Both sexes have white band across bill. Name refers to male's obscure brown collar. Nests on ponds and marshy lakes and in bogs. Winters on fresh water.

RUDDY DUCK *Oxyura jamaicensis*. 15" (39 cm). A small, compact duck with a unique stiff-tailed silhouette. Breeding male is unmistakable. Female and winter male told by their shape, dark caps, and pale cheeks (striped on female). Common summer resident of freshwater marshes and prairie sloughs. Winters also on coastal waters and saltmarshes.

DIVING DUCKS I

Canvasback

Scaup

CANVASBACK

male

female

male

REDHEAD

female

female

LESSER SCAUP

male

male

GREATER SCAUP

male

RING-NECKED
DUCK

female

female

breeding
male

RUDDY DUCK

winter male

BUFFLEHEAD *Bucephala albeola*. 14" (36 cm). Small and compact. Male has flashy white sides and puffy head patch. Female is dusky gray with a small white cheek spot. Buffleheads nest in tree cavities near lakes and rivers of northern forests. They are common migrants and winter residents on open water throughout the East. When surfacing from a dive, Buffleheads seem to pop buoyantly from the water. In winter, compare with similarly sized Horned Grebe (p. 26) and Ruddy Duck (p. 38).

COMMON GOLDENEYE *Bucephala clangula*. 18½" (47 cm). Compact sea duck with a chunky head and pale yellow eyes. Male's glossy blackish-green head has a conspicuous round white spot near the base of the bill. Female grayish with chocolate-brown head. Locally common in winter along the coast and on open lakes and rivers. Nesting habits similar to those of the Bufflehead. **Barrow's Goldeneye**, a rare winter visitor to the North Atlantic coast, has a crescent-shaped face spot and black bar on side of breast (females of the two species are nearly identical). The similarly patterned mergansers are sleeker, with long, narrow bills.

HOODED MERGANSER *Lophodytes cucullatus*. 18" (46 cm). Male is unmistakable, but note that he can raise or lower his crest, thereby greatly altering his profile. Female is dark, with narrow bill and bushy brownish crest. Similar to the nondiving Wood Duck in habitat and nest-site preferences; in fact, females of both have been known to lay eggs in each other's nests!

RED-BREASTED MERGANSER *Mergus serrator*. 22½" (58 cm). Elongated and slender, with narrow red bill and shaggy, unkempt crest. Male's brownish breast is diagnostic. Identifying female mergansers requires practice. Hooded is smaller and darker, while Common is heftier, with a trim, cleaner-looking plumage. Common in winter along the coast; the only merganser likely to be seen on salt water.

COMMON MERGANSER *Mergus merganser*. 24½" (63 cm). Large and sleek. Male has a blackish uncrested head and peach-tinged white sides and breast. Female resembles the Red-breasted, but note the crisp delineation between the neck and breast and the well-defined white chin patch. Nests along wooded streams, rivers, and lakeshores; fairly common in winter on open lakes and rivers.

DIVING DUCKS II

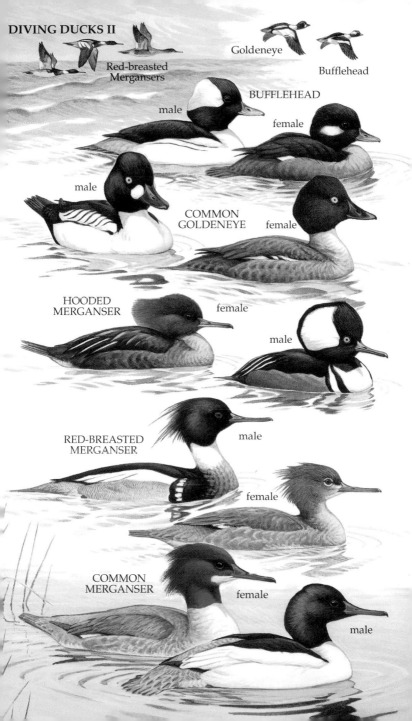

Goldeneye

Bufflehead

Red-breasted
Mergansers

BUFFLEHEAD

male

female

male

COMMON
GOLDENEYE

female

HOODED
MERGANSER

female

male

RED-BREASTED
MERGANSER

male

female

COMMON
MERGANSER

female

male

OLDSQUAW *Clangula hyemalis.* Male 22" (56 cm), female 16" (41 cm). Male's long-tailed profile and bold pattern are unique; note the dusky face patch on white head and neck. Female also has a head paler than that of other sea ducks, with a dark ear patch. Locally common in winter on the Great Lakes and Atlantic coast (rare south of the Carolinas). Oldsquaws molt into distinctive but rarely seen breeding plumages; they nest on the Arctic tundra.

SURF SCOTER *Melanitta perspicillata.* 19½" (50 cm). Dark and heavy-bodied, with a stout beak. Male has a multicolored bill and odd white patches on his crown and nape. Female scoters may be difficult to identify. Surf has two pale face patches, like the White-winged, but lacks its wing patches and has a dark cap. The less common **Black Scoter** female (not shown) has a pale face and throat, with a dark crown and nape. The male Black is identified by the bright orange knob on the base of his bill. The rare **Harlequin Duck**, which also has pale spots on its face, is much smaller, with a stubby bill. In winter, Surf Scoters are fairly common offshore (rare on the Great Lakes), often seen in mixed rafts with other sea ducks. Like most sea ducks, they nest in the Arctic.

WHITE-WINGED SCOTER *Melanitta fusca.* 21" (54 cm). Dark and heavy-bodied, with white wing patches that are conspicuous in flight and sometimes visible on the sides of swimming birds. Male has a small white mark next to his eye (noticeable even from far away) and an orange patch and black knob on his bill. Female most easily told by her wing patches. A winter visitor to the East, primarily offshore.

COMMON EIDER *Somateria mollissima.* 24" (61 cm). Large, stocky duck with a sloping forehead. Adult male's white back and black sides are unmistakable. Young male is mostly dark with a white breast. Female is mottled brown, warmer in color than female scoters and lacking their pale facial markings. (Black Ducks, occasionally seen offshore, have thin necks, rounded heads, and flattened, spatulate bills; they do not dive.) Eiders are year-round residents of rocky North Atlantic coasts. In summer they are seen only as far south as southern Maine. In winter they gather offshore in large rafts, locally south to Long Island, New York. The much rarer **King Eider** has a blocky-shaped head with a steep forehead. Adult males are told by their black back, orange forehead patch, and pink bill.

Common
Eider

Surf Scoter

White-winged Scoter

Oldsquaw

male

female

OLDSQUAW

female

SURF SCOTER

male

WHITE-WINGED
SCOTER

female

male

BLACK SCOTER

male

immature
male

COMMON EIDER

female

male

DIVING AND SEA DUCKS

BIRDS OF PREY These birds are also known as *raptors* or *hawks*. The term typically refers to several related groups of diurnal (day-flying) carnivores, including vultures, kites, accipiters, eagles and buteos, harriers, falcons, and ospreys. (Owls, although also predatory, are not related. See pp. 86 to 89.) Hawks are highly variable in plumage and females of many species are considerably larger than males. Although raptor identification is daunting for beginners, the key is to become thoroughly familiar with the most common hawks of each type. Then similar species can be judged in comparison. With practice, even a silhouetted bird soaring high above can be identified by observing overall size and shape; the relative proportions of wings, tail, and head; the attitude of wings when soaring; or the sequence of wing flaps and glides when in flight.

TURKEY VULTURE *Cathartes aura*. 29" (74 cm). Wingspan 6' (1.8 m). Large, brownish-black with a featherless reddish head; immature has dusky head. Undersides of the wings are two-toned; silvery flight feathers contrast with darker wing linings. Comparable in size only to eagles, Turkey Vultures in flight appear long-tailed and small-headed. They teeter buoyantly on rising currents of sun-warmed air (*thermals*), with wings angled upward in a pronounced *V* (called a *dihedral*)—a shape recognizable from great distances. Most often seen searching for carrion, singly or in small groups over highways and fields and along ridges and hillsides. Common; recently extended its range northward.

BLACK VULTURE *Coragyps atratus*. 25" (58 cm). Wingspan 5' (1.5 m). Black with a grayish naked head. Smaller, darker, and more compact than Turkey Vulture, with a shorter tail. In flight, tends to soar less often, with quick, shallow wingbeats and short glides. Note the pale patch at the base of the primary flight feathers. Locally common near towns, it often gathers in large flocks. In the process of expanding its range to the Northeast.

BALD EAGLE *Haliaeetus leucocephalus*. 35" (90 cm). Wingspan almost 7' (2 m). Adults unmistakable, but young birds (to 4 years) are dark with lighter blotches and may be confused with the rare **Golden Eagle** (not shown). Flight profile of the Bald Eagle is distinct. Note the large head, heavy beak, and long wings held horizontally. Although still endangered in the East, Bald Eagles have recently increased in number. Seen most often in winter along the shores of reservoirs, rivers, and coasts. Common in parts of Florida.

VULTURES AND EAGLES

wings held in
shallow V

TURKEY
VULTURE

BLACK
VULTURE

wings held flat

BALD
EAGLE

first-year
immature

OSPREY *Pandion haliaetus.* 23" (59 cm). Wingspan almost 6' (1.8 m). Large; dark above and white below. White head with dark mask. Heavily streaked underwing pattern with dark mark at wrist is diagnostic, as is flight profile, with outer halves of long, arched wings angled backward, forming a distinct "crook." Recovering now from past pesticide poisonings, the Osprey is again becoming a common summer resident of coastal marshes and northern lakes and rivers, where it builds oversized nests atop dead trees, telephone poles, or elevated platforms. Ospreys eat fish, diving with talons outstretched to snatch them from the water.

MISSISSIPPI KITE *Ictinia mississippiensis.* 14" (38 cm). A sleek raptor with long, pointed wings and a long, narrow tail, this species is ashy gray, palest on the head. Its wings have distinctive white patches on the secondaries, visible in flight. The tip of its unbarred black tail is squared or slightly notched. Graceful and leisurely in flight, Mississippi Kites feed predominantly on insects and are often seen in small flocks hawking them over golf courses, prairie shelterbelts (windbreaks), and bottomland forests. Local within their mapped range but spreading; most common in southern plains states.

AMERICAN SWALLOW-TAILED KITE *Elanoides forficatus.* 24" (60 cm). A striking raptor of southeastern swamps, marshes, and bottomlands; formerly more widespread, now quite local; though most numerous in Florida. Swallow-tailed Kites feed on frogs, reptiles, and large insects, which they often catch and consume in flight. These aerial acrobats may hunt in small groups.

NORTHERN HARRIER *Circus cyaneus.* 20" (52 cm). Long-limbed and lanky, the "marsh hawk" skims buoyantly low over dunes, marshes, prairies, and farmland, wings held in a pronounced V and white rump flashing. Adult males are pale gray with black wing tips; females are considerably larger, streaked, and brownish. Immature plumage is similar to female's, with unstreaked cinnamon underparts. In the northern states, wintering Rough-legged Hawks (p. 48) also fly low and flash white on the tail, but they have a bold underwing pattern. In the Florida Everglades, Harriers may be confused with the rare **Snail Kite**, which is darker and has more white at the base of the tail. During migration, Harriers often soar high up, like buteos, but may be told by their distinctive shape.

nest platform

carrying fish

OSPREY

MISSISSIPPI KITE

immature
soaring

AMERICAN
SWALLOW-TAILED
KITE

NORTHERN
HARRIER

female

male

OSPREY, KITES, AND HARRIER

BUTEOS With broad wings and tails, buteos are exquisitely designed for soaring. They are best represented by the Red-tailed Hawk, our most widespread and familiar raptor. Typical adult buteos are fairly easy to identify, but some species occur also in dark morphs or have confusing subspecies. These variants, as well as immatures, are very difficult to distinguish.

RED-TAILED HAWK *Buteo jamaicensis*. 22" (56 cm). Wingspan 4' (1.2 m). In the East a large pale-breasted hawk perched on a roadside snag is almost always this species. Note the band of streaks across the belly, and the adult's rusty tail (paler underneath). Immatures have narrowly barred brownish tails and are easily confused with other young buteos. Call is a shrill, screeching *keeeeer*. The **Rough-legged Hawk**, a winter visitor to prairies, marshes, and other open country, has a white tail with a dark terminal band. The most commonly seen plumage is pale-headed with a dark belly and broad blackish wrist patches. Unlike other buteos, it often hovers.

BROAD-WINGED HAWK *Buteo platypterus*. 16" (41 cm). Crow-sized and compact. The short tail is broadly banded with black and white (only one visible white band). The undersides of the wings are white with a dark margin. Common summer resident of mixed woodlands. In autumn, Broad-wings migrate in large soaring flocks (called *kettles*) following mountain ridges, river valleys, and coasts south into the tropics. Call is a high-pitched monotone whistle, usually two notes: *see-eeee*.

RED-SHOULDERED HAWK *Buteo lineatus*. 20" (52 cm). A slender buteo of deciduous woodlands and swamps. Adult is barred reddish below, with a rusty shoulder, and has a fairly long dark tail with narrow white bars. Soaring birds often show a translucent crescent-shaped "window" across the primaries. Uncommon in the Northeast but common and conspicuous in the South. Florida adults are noticeably paler than northern birds. Call is a loud, jaylike *kee-yar*.

SWAINSON'S HAWK *Buteo swainsoni*. 20½" (53 cm). Common summer resident of open plains and prairies, this buteo is best told by its long, pointed wings and, in the predominant light morph, by its dark chest and pale belly. In flight, Swainson's can also be told by the dark undersides of the flight feathers and pale wing linings. Like Broad-wings, Swainson's Hawks migrate in crowded, soaring flocks to winter in South America.

BUTEOS

ED-TAILED
HAWK

immature

Red-tailed

adults

Broad-winged

RED-SHOULDERED
HAWK

Florida
subspecies

Red-shouldered

Swainson's

SWAINSON'S
HAWK

light morph
adult

Rough-legged

ACCIPITERS With short, rounded wings and long tails, accipiters are adapted for swift maneuvering within dense forests. Their flight typically consists of a few swift flaps followed by a short sail, though they may ocassionally soar. Accipiters prey mostly on other birds and small mammals. Separating the three North American species, especially as immatures, is a challenge even for experts, who look for subtle differences in the birds' shapes and proportions. Size alone is an unreliable field mark, due to the wide divergence in size between males and females of each species.

SHARP-SHINNED HAWK *Accipiter striatus.* 12" (31 cm). A small, slender raptor; fairly common in mixed woodlands. Appears smaller-headed and shorter-tailed than the very similar but larger **Cooper's Hawk**. Also note the shapes of their tails: on the Sharp-shinned the tip is square or slightly notched; on Cooper's the tail is long, rounded, and tipped with white. The rare **Northern Goshawk** is massive, and more likely to be mistaken for a buteo than for another accipiter. Adult Goshawk is blue-gray above, pale gray below, and has a bold white eyebrow.

FALCONS Bullet-shaped with tapered wings and narrow tails, falcons are speed demons. When diving ("stooping") down on its prey, the Peregrine Falcon can reach speeds of almost 100 miles per hour! Falcons fly with steady, deliberate wingbeats. They may also soar with wings and tails spread wide, but their wings always appear pointed.

AMERICAN KESTREL *Falco sparverius.* 10" (25 cm). Formerly called Sparrow Hawk. Small; in both sexes the striped face and rusty tail are diagnostic. This is our most widespread and familiar falcon; inhabits road-sides and open country, where it is often seen perched on power lines or hovering in midair with wings beating rapidly. Kestrels eat insects and small rodents.

MERLIN *Falco columbarius.* 12" (31 cm). Formerly called Pigeon Hawk. Darker and more robust than the Kestrel, with a boldly barred tail and no dark facial stripes. Male is dark slate above; female, dark brown. Uncommon migrant and rare winter resident of open country.

PEREGRINE FALCON *Falco peregrinus.* 18" (45 cm). Crow-sized, with a distinctive dark "helmet." Nearly wiped out by 1950 in the East; captive-bred birds have been successfully reintroduced in the wild. Though still endangered, Peregrines can be seen nesting on city skyscrapers and suspension bridges. Along the East Coast, small numbers (from Arctic populations) are also seen as fall migrants.

ACCIPITERS AND FALCONS

SHARP-SHINNED HAWK

adult female

immature male

male

female

COOPER'S HAWK

AMERICAN KESTREL

Kestrel

female

MERLIN

male

adult

immature

adult

PEREGRINE FALCON

WOOD STORK *Mycteria americana*. 40" (103 cm). A huge white wading bird with a dark featherless head and neck and black flight feathers and tail. Immature has a pale bill and dusky-feathered head. In flight, the neck is extended, with long legs trailing behind (compare with White Pelican, p. 30). This is North America's only stork; restricted to Florida and southeastern coastal swamps, although a few may wander north and inland in late summer.

ROSEATE SPOONBILL *Ajaia ajaja*. 32" (82 cm). Unmistakable pink and white wading bird, with a unique long, flattened "spoonbill." Adults have a grayish-green featherless head. Immatures are pale pinkish overall. They feed by sweeping their bills back and forth through the shallows, sifting out crustaceans and small fish. A local resident of southern Florida and the Gulf Coast.

WHITE IBIS *Eudocimus albus*. 25" (64 cm). Adult is white with a long, down-curved red bill, and black wing tips (conspicuous in flight). Immature is brownish with white belly and rump. A locally common and gregarious resident of southeastern wetlands; small numbers (especially of young birds) may wander far north of the mapped range in late summer.

GLOSSY IBIS *Plegadis falcinellus*. 23" (59 cm). A dark, slender wader with a long, down-curved bill. In good light, breeding adult is chestnut with a bronzed, purple sheen; winter bird is duller bronze with a finely streaked head. In flight, the extended neck separates this species from dark herons, while the trailing legs and curved bill distinguish it from cormorants. Common and widespread on coastal marshes and inlets. Along the Texas coast and inland on the Great Plains wetlands, it is replaced by the closely related **White-faced Ibis**, which is nearly identical. In breeding plumage, the White-faced has red legs, red eyes, and a white margin bordering its red face.

LIMPKIN *Aramus guarauna*. 26½" (68 cm). An odd, long-legged relative of rails and cranes. Plumage is brown with pale streaks and spots, suggesting a young Night-Heron (p. 54), but its neck is tall and slender, its bill long and slightly down-curved. Limpkins fly with their necks extended. An uncommon and reclusive resident of swamps and freshwater marshes in Florida and southeastern Georgia.

Wood Stork

Spoonbill

White Ibis

adult

immature

Glossy
Ibis

ROSEATE
SPOONBILL

WOOD
STORK

adult

immature

adult

WHITE
IBIS

immature

breeding

GLOSSY
IBIS

LIMPKIN

MISCELLANEOUS LONG-LEGGED WADERS

HERONS, EGRETS, AND BITTERNS All of these belong to the same family of long-legged waders. Egrets are generally white; bitterns are stocky, with shorter legs. All have daggerlike beaks to grab or spear their prey. Unlike other similarly shaped wading birds, herons fly with their necks folded in a tight S. Several species may nest together with ibis or storks in crowded treetop colonies called *rookeries*. After breeding, some species may wander outside their mapped range.

LEAST BITTERN *Ixobrychus exilis*. 13" (33 cm). A tiny heron with pale buff wing patches. Fairly common but reclusive summer resident of freshwater or brackish marshes. Usually seen flying just above the top of the marsh grass, then dropping down again out of sight. Compare to similarly sized rails (p. 62).

AMERICAN BITTERN *Botaurus lentiginosus*. 27" (62 cm). Cinnamon-colored, streaked with pale buff below; note the dark slash on each side of the neck, pale eyebrow, and, in flight, two-toned wings. Common but secretive; when disturbed, Bitterns "freeze"—with their beak pointed upward—and blend into the surrounding reeds. During breeding season their call, a liquid, "pumping" *oonk-a-loonk*, often reveals their presence.

GREEN HERON *Butorides virescens*. 19" (49 cm). A small, crow-sized heron. At a distance, appears all dark with bright orange legs; but in good light, note rich maroon neck and pale blue-green back. Immatures are streaked below. A common and widespread summer resident of most wetland habitats, including wooded streams and ponds. Typically solitary.

BLACK-CROWNED NIGHT-HERON *Nycticorax nycticorax*. 25" (64 cm). Stocky, short-legged heron (in flight, toes barely protrude behind tail). Adult is distinctive, but gray-brown immature, spotted and streaked with white, resembles young Yellow-crowned Night-Heron or tawnier American Bittern. Common resident of coastal swamps and marshes; locally common inland. Night-Herons forage most actively at dusk and during the night.

YELLOW-CROWNED NIGHT-HERON *Nyctanassa violacea*. 24½" (63 cm). Similar to Black-crowned in size, shape, and habits. Adult identified by clean gray underparts, black-and-white-streaked back, and bold head pattern. Immature resembles Black-crowned, but can be told by its longer legs (in flight, entire foot trails behind tail), stout blackish bill, and grayer, more finely spotted plumage. Common in the Southeast.

HERONS AND BITTERNS

Green

Black-crowned
adult

immature

female

LEAST
BITTERN

male

Least

American

AMERICAN
BITTERN

GREEN HERON

adult

BLACK-CROWNED NIGHT-HERON

immature

YELLOW-
CROWNED
NIGHT-HERON

adult

TRICOLORED HERON *Egretta tricolor*. 26" (66 cm). Formerly named Louisiana Heron. Medium-sized, lean, and lanky heron; slate-blue with a white belly. Very common resident of southeastern coastal marshes and mangroves, this seemingly hyperactive heron often wades thigh-deep, jabbing its lancelike bill at minnows and other prey.

LITTLE BLUE HERON *Egretta caerulea*. 24½" (63 cm). Adults appear all dark; shorter-billed than Tricoloreds. Immatures are white and very similar to Snowy Egrets. Look for their greenish legs, gray lores, and black-tipped gray bills. As the birds mature, they may become pied, with dark blotches on white plumage. A common, widespread heron of coasts and wetlands. Along the Gulf Coast, this species might be confused with the rarer **Reddish Egret**, which occurs in both a dark morph and an all-white form. In breeding plumage, Reddish Egrets can be told by their distinctive black-tipped pink bills, and long, shaggy neck feathers.

CATTLE EGRET *Bubulcus ibis*. 20" (51 cm). A small, compact egret with a short yellow bill. In breeding plumage, the crown, breast, and back are tinged with orange. True to its name, this heron often follows large grazing mammals, such as cattle, snatching insects and other prey that are flushed from the grass. Cattle Egrets were originally found only in southern Europe and Africa but recently have spread to every continent. They are still expanding their range in North America. May occur in any open grassy or wet habitat.

GREAT EGRET *Casmerodius albus*. 39" (100 cm). Extremely tall and slender, with black legs and feet and a yellow bill. Common and widespread, this is our largest white heron, except in southern Florida, where the rare "Great White" Heron (a form of the Great Blue Heron, p. 58) is found. Great Egrets wade with slow, measured grace. Egrets were nearly wiped out earlier in this century, shot for their delicate breeding plumes, or *aigrettes*, which were used to adorn hats.

SNOWY EGRET *Egretta thula*. 24" (61 cm). Slender, medium-sized egret with a thin black bill, black legs, and bright yellow feet and lores. Immatures may show yellow extending up the backs of the legs. Very active foragers, they rush about, stirring up bottom muck with their feet. Common, but limited mostly to coastal marshes and estuaries; more widespread in the South.

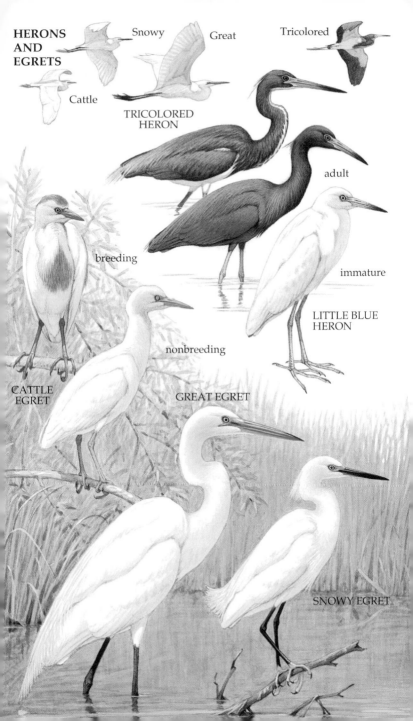

HERONS AND EGRETS

Snowy

Great

Tricolored

Cattle

TRICOLORED HERON

breeding

adult

immature

LITTLE BLUE HERON

nonbreeding

CATTLE EGRET

GREAT EGRET

SNOWY EGRET

GREAT BLUE HERON *Ardea herodias*. 48½" (124 cm). Huge. Bluish-gray with tan neck and white head; in breeding adults, black eyebrow trails into a wispy crest. Our largest heron, this so-called crane has a posture different from that of true cranes. A Great Blue typically holds its neck bent in an open S, though it can also tuck it in tightly or stretch it upright. Appears dark and eagle-sized in flight, with slow, steady wingbeats; but note the trailing legs and folded neck. Common and widespread. Usually nests in small colonies by wooded swamps; may be found other times near almost any salt or fresh water. In the Florida Keys, the resident white morph, called the "Great White" Heron, can be told from the smaller Great Egret by its yellowish legs.

SANDHILL CRANE *Grus canadensis*. 43" (110 cm). A tall gray wader. Note the red crown and bushy tuft of plumes on the rear end. Immature is brownish, and lacks the crown patch. Cranes fly with their necks extended and migrate in high-flying V-shaped formations, like geese. In winter they congregate in huge, noisy flocks on open fields, prairies, and marshes. A second North American crane species, the very rare **Whooping Crane**, is larger than the Sandhill; it is white with black wing tips and a red face patch. Now recovering from near extinction, a small population nests in central Canada and winters at Aransas National Wildlife Refuge in coastal Texas.

GAMEBIRDS In a general sense, all birds that are hunted are referred to as "game," but technically speaking, the group includes only turkeys, grouse, quail, and pheasants—mostly squat, chicken-like birds that scratch and peck on the ground for seeds and insects. They have stout legs and claws, stubby beaks, and short, rounded wings that allow for quick getaways, but not sustained flight. When flushed, they usually land nearby in a concealed spot. Courting males are often flamboyant in their mating displays and behavior.

WILD TURKEY *Meleagris gallopavo*. Male 48" (123 cm), female 36" (93 cm). Unmistakable. Resembles its barnyard descendants except in temperament. Wild birds are wary and furtive. Flocks of Wild Turkeys once ranged throughout the East but were nearly exterminated by overhunting. Recently reintroduced to parts of their former range, they have become quite common in spots. Look for them in open deciduous woodlands and listen for the familiar *gobble-gobble*.

HERON, CRANES, AND TURKEY

Great Blue Heron

Sandhill Crane

Whooping Crane

immature

GREAT BLUE HERON

Whooping Crane with Sandhills

SANDHILL CRANE

male

female

courtship display

WILD TURKEY

male

GRAY PARTRIDGE *Perdix perdix*. 12½" (32 cm). Pigeon-sized; finely barred grayish-brown with cinnamon face and outer tail feathers. Note chestnut belly patch. Introduced from Europe in the last century, now locally well established in open farmlands.

NORTHERN BOBWHITE *Colinus virginianus*. 10" (25 cm). Small, plump, and short-tailed, with pale throat and eyebrow. Resident of fields and brushy edges, this well-camouflaged quail often betrays itself by its whistled *bob-white?* call. During most of the year, Bobwhites forage and roost in small flocks called *coveys*, which, when flushed, explode from the brush in every direction. Abundant in the South; scarce along the northern perimeter of its range. In the arid scrubland of Texas and the southwestern Great Plains, it occurs with the distinctive **Scaled Quail,** which is bluish-gray and has a conspicuous white-tufted crest.

RUFFED GROUSE *Bonasa umbellus*. 17" (44 cm). Common, chicken-sized gamebird of forests and brushy clearings. Note the rusty or grayish fan-shaped tail with bold black band. Courtship display is rarely seen, though often heard. Males spread their tails, puff their neck ruff, and beat their wings in an accelerating flutter, generating a deep, muffled, drumming sound. In spruce forests of Canada and northern border states, this species is replaced by the **Spruce Grouse**, which may be identified by its shorter dark, rust-tipped tail.

SHARP-TAILED GROUSE *Tympanuchus phasianellus*. 17½" (45 cm). Locally common in northern prairies, grasslands, and open brush. Note especially the elongated tail that flashes white in flight. The closely related **Greater** and **Lesser Prairie-Chickens** are rare and local residents of remnant patches of prairie in the central and southern plains. They are heavily barred below (rather than lightly streaked) and have short dark tails. In spring, males gather in traditional communal courtship arenas called *leks*, where they strut and display to attract hens.

RING-NECKED PHEASANT *Phasianus colchicus*. Male 33" (86 cm), female 22" (56 cm). Large and long-tailed. Male is unmistakable. Female is larger and longer-tailed than other grouse or Prairie-Chickens. Native to Asia, this species was originally imported from Europe to stock fields for hunting. It is now common and widespread in open fields, farmland, and even urban parks.

GAMEBIRDS

GRAY PARTRIDGE

Pheasant

females in flight

Sharp-tailed

Ruffed

NORTHERN BOBWHITE

female

male

red morph

RUFFED GROUSE

male displaying ruffs

gray morph

male

SHARP-TAILED GROUSE

female

courtship display

RING-NECKED PHEASANT

male

female

RAILS AND GALLINULES Chickenlike marsh birds with stubby tails and long, slender toes, rails can compress their bodies to become "as thin as a rail" as they skulk through dense vegetation. They are notoriously secretive, though most species are quite vocal. In the same family, gallinules (or moorhens) and coots are more easily seen scooting about on floating plants or swimming in open water. All members of this family have short, rounded wings and seldom fly; paradoxically, some species migrate long distances.

CLAPPER RAIL *Rallus longirostris.* 15" (38 cm). A large, grayish, long-billed rail of salt marshes. Common and among the easier rails to see. Listen for its dry, staccato cackle, *kek kek kek kek kek*, emanating from coastal wetlands. The nearly identical **King Rail** is somewhat rustier and prefers inland freshwater marshes.

VIRGINIA RAIL *Rallus limicola.* 9½" (24.5 cm). A small, dark, long-billed rail. (Clapper and King are similarly shaped but much larger.) Commonly nests in swamps and on freshwater marshes; in winter also inhabits salt marshes. Calls include a series of dry notes, *kick kick kidick kidick kidick*, and odd, piglike grunts.

SORA *Porzana carolina.* 9" (22 cm). Common and widespread on freshwater marshes but secretive; still, the only small short-billed rail likely to be seen. Note the adult's black face and yellowish bill. Immature is tinged brownish and lacks the adult's mask.

AMERICAN COOT *Fulica americana.* 15" (39 cm). Mouse-gray with a blackish head and conspicuous white bill. Immature has a pale grayish head and a dingy white bill. Common on marshes, ponds, and, in winter, open water. Often seen swimming with other waterfowl; note the Coot's dumpy shape, small head, and chickenlike bill. Coots nod their heads when they swim and spatter across the water as they take flight.

COMMON MOORHEN *Gallinula chloropus.* 13½" (35 cm). Also known as Common Gallinule. Slate-gray with a yellow-tipped red bill and frontal shield (an extension of the bill onto the forehead); note the white undertail patches and stripe along the flanks. Immature is browner and has a dark bill. Common and widespread, the Moorhen wades along marshy edges, walks on floating vegetation, or swims, bobbing its head as it paddles. In the Southeast, the similarly shaped **Purple Gallinule** is easily identified by its purplish-blue and green plumage.

RAILS AND
GALLINULES

CLAPPER
RAIL

VIRGINIA
RAIL

SORA

Coot

immature

Moorhen

adult

adult

AMERICAN
COOT

immature

COMMON
MOORHEN

PURPLE
GALLINULE

PLOVERS Plump shorebirds with round heads and short, stubby bills, plovers scurry about like wind-up toys, pausing stiffly between each dash. When poised, they seem to vanish: their camouflaged upperparts and boldly patterned breasts help mask their shape—a phenomenon called *disruptive coloration*. Like other waders, plovers are most abundant during migration, when they congregate in large flocks on shores, mud flats, marshes, and farmland. Black-bellied and Semipalmated Plovers are also common winter residents of the South Atlantic and Gulf coasts.

BLACK-BELLIED PLOVER *Pluvialis squatarola.* 11½" (30 cm). Large plover with a stout beak. Unmistakable in breeding plumage; winter adults are dull grayish and best told by their distinctive shape, white rumps, and striking black "armpits" (called *axillaries*, visible in flight). Molting birds with black blotches on their bellies are common during migration. Juveniles in fresh plumage (primarily in fall) have a buff-tinged, checkered pattern on their backs and are often mistaken for the very similar **American Golden-Plover** in its winter plumage. The Golden-Plover, a regular fall transient along the Atlantic coast and a common spring migrant on midwestern prairies and the Gulf Coast, is smaller, darker, and tinged with golden buff above. It has a small delicate bill, a dark rump, and pale axillaries. The Black-bellied's call is a whistled *plee-u-wee*.

KILLDEER *Charadrius vociferus.* 10" (26 cm). A slender plover, told by its double breast bands, tawny rump, and fairly long tail. Widespread and conspicuous, especially in cultivated fields and pastures; often seen far from water, nesting even on gravel rooftops. Its call is a loud, shrill *kill-deer*, repeated continuously.

SEMIPALMATED PLOVER *Charadrius semipalmatus.* 7" (18 cm). Small; mud-colored above, with a single breast band. Common migrant, often in large flocks on shores and mud flats. The **Piping Plover**, an uncommon and declining species of coastal dunes and beaches, dry lakeshores, and sandbars, is sand-colored above.

RUDDY TURNSTONE *Arenaria interpres.* 9" (23 cm). A squat, ploverlike sandpiper, with a short, pointed bill, dark chest patch, and flashy harlequin pattern. A common migrant and winter resident of coastal beaches, rocky shores, and jetties, where it probes among pebbles for food. During migration, may also occur on the shores of the Great Lakes. Often flocks with Sanderlings, Dunlin, or Purple Sandpipers (p. 72).

PLOVERS AND TURNSTONE

nonbreeding

breeding

nonbreeding

Black-bellied Plovers

Ruddy Turnstone

nonbreeding

American Golden-Plover

nonbreeding

BLACK-BELLIED PLOVER

nonbreeding

juvenile

Killdeer by its nest feigning injury to distract a predator

breeding

AMERICAN GOLDEN-PLOVER

breeding

KILLDEER

SEMIPALMATED PLOVER

breeding

RUDDY TURNSTONE

nonbreeding

nonbreeding

breeding

PIPING PLOVER

breeding

SHOREBIRDS A diverse group of waders, most shorebirds have long legs and long, slender bills they use to probe the shallows and mud for invertebrates. Many species nest in the Arctic and occur in the East only as migrants, pausing to refuel during their spring flight northward, and again on their return passage in late summer and fall. They gather in large mixed flocks on shores, mud flats, and wetlands. Some are also found inland on prairies and farmland. Shorebirds include plovers (p. 64), avocets, stilts, oystercatchers, and all types of sandpipers (turnstones, godwits, yellowlegs, etc.). Of the numerous tiny sandpipers, called "peeps," which are very difficult to identify, only the two most common species are included.

AMERICAN AVOCET *Recurvirostra americana*. 18" (46 cm). Tall, graceful wader with a delicate upturned bill and striking pied wing pattern. Avocets may forage in flocks, sweeping their bills back and forth just beneath the water's surface. They nest around inland brackish lakes or on prairie marshes and winter on coastal marshes. An occasional fall migrant on the East coast.

BLACK-NECKED STILT *Himantopus mexicanus*. 14½" (37 cm). A slender, delicate wader, boldly patterned in black and white, with long bright pink legs. Forages in marshy shallows bordering prairie lakes, sloughs, and coastal estuaries. Has recently extended its coastal breeding range northward.

AMERICAN OYSTERCATCHER *Haematopus palliatus*. 18½" (47 cm). A large red beak, bright yellow eyes, and pied plumage give this heavyset wader a clownlike expression. Found locally on coastal beaches and mud flats from Texas north to Massachusetts. Immatures have dusky-tipped bills.

WHIMBREL *Numenius phaeopus*. 17" (44 cm). Large waders with long, down-curved bills are called curlews. The Whimbrel is the only curlew likely to be seen in the Northeast, where it is a fairly common migrant. Winters along southern coasts. Note striped crown and grayish brown tones. The larger **Long-billed Curlew**, told by its warm buff plumage, cinnamon wing linings, and extremely long bill, nests in grasslands of the upper Great Plains and winters mostly along the Texas coast.

MARBLED GODWIT *Limosa fedoa*. 18" (46 cm). Godwits are large waders with long, upturned bills. The Marbled is warm buff with cinnamon wing linings, much like the Long-billed Curlew, but note the diagnostic shape and bright pink base of its bill. Nests on prairie wetlands, wintering along the coast.

SHOREBIRDS I

Oystercatcher

Whimbrel

Stilt

Marbled Godwit

Avocet

AMERICAN
AVOCET

breeding

nonbreeding

BLACK-NECKED
STILT

AMERICAN
OYSTERCATCHER

WHIMBREL

MARBLED
GODWIT

LONG-BILLED
CURLEW

UPLAND SANDPIPER *Bartramia longicauda.* 12" (30 cm). An oddly shaped shorebird of prairies, pastures, grassy fields, and airports. Note the full belly, long neck, and small head with large eyes. Most easily seen when perched above grass on a fence or post. Fairly common in appropriate habitat; rare migrant along the East Coast.

SHORT-BILLED DOWITCHER *Limnodromus griseus.* 11" (28 cm). Common; a stocky sandpiper with a long, straight bill. Typically wades thigh-deep with head down, bill probing for food. During migration, dowitchers gather in large flocks on marshes and mud flats. They winter along the Gulf and Atlantic coasts, north to Virginia. Within a flock, plumages may vary widely according to age, molt, and subspecies variations. Such flocks often include the nearly identical **Long-billed Dowitcher**, a common migrant in the Midwest and regular fall transient in the East; common in the South during winter. The two species are often indistinguishable in winter except by their calls (Short-billed, a soft *tu-tu-tu*; Long-billed, a high, sharp *keek*). Both have a white rump and lower back, visible in flight as a pale wedge between dark wings. Yellowlegs (p. 70) are taller, with bright yellow legs. The solitary Snipe favors a different habitat.

COMMON SNIPE *Gallinago gallinago.* 11" (28 cm). An inland sandpiper with a short neck, squat legs, and a long, straight bill. Note the boldly striped crown and back. Common in upland habitats, such as wet pastures, bogs, and prairie potholes; rare on coastal salt marshes. Usually solitary and well camouflaged, Snipes are most easily seen when flushed, bursting from the grass in a fast, darting flight and emitting a raspy "scraping" note.

AMERICAN WOODCOCK *Scolopax minor.* 11" (28 cm). A squat, pigeon-sized shorebird of woodland edges and moist thickets. Note its short neck; large eye; long, heavy beak; and rich, tawny plumage. Perfectly camouflaged against woodland leaf litter, Woodcocks are rarely seen except when flushed. Compared with Snipes, they have dumpier silhouettes, more rounded wings, and less erratic flight. In early spring, twilight courtship displays high above clearings and meadows include spectacular dives, an audible twittering of wings, and a nasal *peeent*.

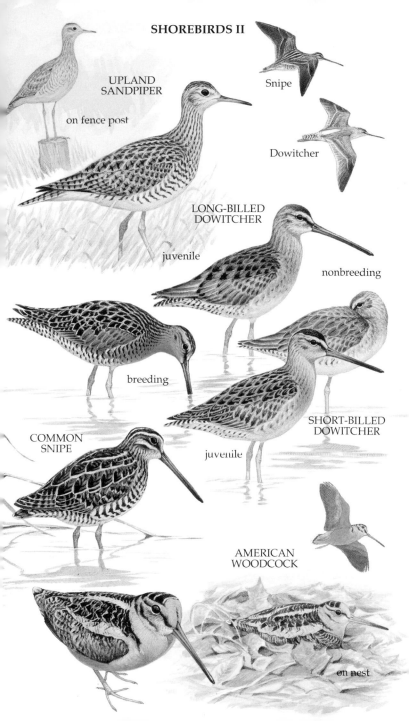

SHOREBIRDS II

UPLAND
SANDPIPER

on fence post

Snipe

Dowitcher

LONG-BILLED
DOWITCHER

juvenile

nonbreeding

breeding

SHORT-BILLED
DOWITCHER

COMMON
SNIPE

juvenile

AMERICAN
WOODCOCK

on nest

WILSON'S PHALAROPE *Phalaropus tricolor.* 9" (23 cm). Phalaropes spin around the water in tight circles, picking at food stirred up in the vortex. (Other shore-birds may wade belly-deep but rarely swim.) Wilson's Phalarope is a delicate shorebird with a long, needle-thin bill. Easily identified in colorful breeding plumage; the male, caring for the young by himself, is duller than the female. Pale grayish in winter. Nests on prairie wet-lands; a rare migrant in the East.

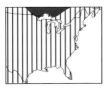

SOLITARY SANDPIPER *Tringa solitaria.* 8½" (21 cm). Dark-backed inland sandpiper with greenish legs and white eye ring. Usually solitary; a fairly common migrant along creeks, ditches, small pools, and lakeshores. Although it sometimes teeters, like the Spotted Sandpiper (which frequents similar habitats), the Solitary is taller and darker, with an all-dark wing.

SPOTTED SANDPIPER *Actitis macularia.* 7½" (19 cm). Small, with short pale legs and dark-tipped bill. Spot-breasted summer plumage unique; nonbreeding bird is plain olive-brown above with white underparts and dusky smudges on the sides of the breast. Walks with body tilted forward, tail constantly bobbing; flies low over water with shallow, quivering wingbeats. Common and widespread in freshwater habitats.

GREATER YELLOWLEGS *Tringa melanoleuca.* 13½" (35 cm). Tall, grayish wader with bright yellow legs. Only the very similar but smaller **Lesser Yellowlegs** has legs as bright. With practice, the two can be told apart by their bills: Lesser's is short, straight, and fine; Greater's is proportionately longer and slightly upturned. Greater's call is an explosive *klew klew klew klew*; Lesser's is less emphatic and consists of only 1 or 2 notes. Note that breeding adults are more heavily marked than the juveniles shown. Both species are common and widespread on shores and marshes. Compare with Dowitchers (p. 68).

WILLET *Catoptrophorus semipalmatus.* 15" (38 cm). Large gray sandpiper of coastal salt marshes; also found on lakeshores, marshes, and wet meadows of the Great Plains. In winter large, noisy flocks gather on beaches of the south Atlantic and Gulf coasts. Note the straight, heavy bill, bluish-gray legs, and flashy wing pattern, revealed in flight. Its varied repetitive calls are loud and shrill: *kip, kip, kip,* or *wee, wee, wee.* Inland nesting Willets are paler than the coastal subspecies shown.

SHOREBIRDS III

nonbreeding

WILSON'S PHALAROPE

breeding female

Willet

Yellowlegs

nonbreeding

SPOTTED SANDPIPER

breeding

SOLITARY SANDPIPER

breeding

GREATER YELLOWLEGS

LESSER YELLOWLEGS

WILLET

nonbreeding

breeding

(Atlantic and Gulf coast subspecies)

RED KNOT *Calidris canutus*. 10½" (27 cm). Plump sandpiper with distinctive ruddy-breasted breeding plumage. Nonbreeding Knots are best told by size and shape. (Sanderling is smaller; similarly sized Dowitchers have much longer bills; Black-bellied Plover has longer legs, plover-shaped head, and stubby bill.) Uncommon migrant; winters on coastal mud flats and beaches locally from Texas to New Jersey.

SANDERLING *Calidris alba*. 8" (20 cm). Small sandpiper of sandy beaches. Often seen scurrying back and forth with the breaking waves; flashes white in the wings when flushed. Late-spring and early-fall migrants in breeding plumage are peppered with black and rust on the foreparts; in winter, silvery gray above (palest of the small sandpipers). Juveniles are checkered with black and white above. Common along Atlantic and Gulf coasts except in midsummer; uncommon migrant on inland lakeshores.

DUNLIN *Calidris alpina*. 8¼" (21 cm). Small sandpiper with moderately long, drooping bill. Black belly patch and rusty back in breeding plumage. In winter, duskier and browner above than Sanderling; slightly larger and longer-billed than "peeps." Common migrant and winter resident of coastal beaches, mud flats, and jetties from Maine to Texas; often flocks with Sanderlings and Turnstones. The **Purple Sandpiper**, which winters only on rocky coasts and jetties of the North Atlantic, might be confused with the Dunlin but is darker purplish-gray with a pale belly, yellowish legs, and dusky bill with a pale base.

SEMIPALMATED SANDPIPER *Calidris pusilla*. 6¼" (16 cm). Sparrow-sized "peep" with black legs and a short black bill. Barely larger than Least, with less streaking below; bill thicker at tip. Common and widespread migrant. Any black-legged, grayish "peep" seen in winter along southern coasts, however, is almost certainly the **Western Sandpiper,** which is also a regular fall migrant along the East Coast. Most Westerns can be told by their longer bill, which droops slightly at the tip, and rusty tinges on the shoulders, crown, and face.

LEAST SANDPIPER *Calidris minutilla*. 6" (15 cm). Tiny brownish "peep" with yellowish or greenish legs and a narrow, tapered bill. Common and widespread; in winter the only "peep" likely to be seen inland.

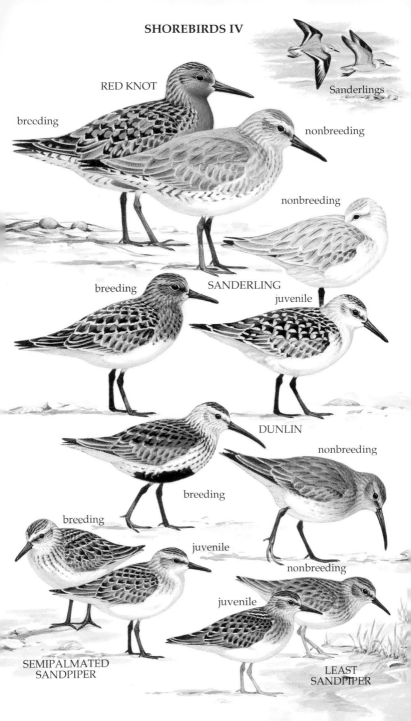

SHOREBIRDS IV

Sanderlings

RED KNOT

breeding

nonbreeding

nonbreeding

SANDERLING

breeding

juvenile

DUNLIN

nonbreeding

breeding

nonbreeding

breeding

juvenile

juvenile

SEMIPALMATED
SANDPIPER

LEAST
SANDPIPER

GULLS Part of a large family that includes terns and skimmers, gulls are strong flyers and buoyant swimmers, with stout, almost hooked bills. Gulls eat almost anything; the larger species are extremely predatory. Unlike terns, gulls do not dive into the surf but swoop down to pluck food from the water. Some species also forage in fields or on prairies. During winter huge flocks gather near harbors, beaches, lakes, garbage dumps, and landfills. Because gulls mature slowly (in 2 to 4 years, with larger gulls tending to take longer), many individuals are immature and can be difficult to identify.

HERRING GULL *Larus argentatus.* 24" (61 cm). A large gull with pale gray back and wings (*mantle*), pink legs, and yellow bill with red spot. First-winter birds are mottled dusky brown and are darker and more evenly toned than other large gulls. They become paler and grayer above with age. Their tails are dark with a whitish base. Try to learn plumages of the Herring Gull, as other gulls are best judged in comparison to this common species. Along the North Atlantic coast or Great Lakes in winter, lighter-colored gulls within a flock of Herring Gulls may be **Iceland Gulls** or **Glaucous Gulls**. Both are ghostly pale in all plumages, with white wing tips.

RING-BILLED GULL *Larus delawarensis.* 19" (49 cm). Smaller and more delicately proportioned than Herring Gull; adult's bill is dull yellow with a complete black ring near the tip, and its legs are greenish-yellow. First-year bird has a bicolored bill (black tip and flesh-colored base) and a narrow dark tail band. A widespread and common gull, especially inland, where it forages and roosts in fields and parking lots. On lakes of the northern Great Plains, this gull nests in large colonies with the **California Gull**, which is identified by its larger size, slightly darker mantle, dark eye, and yellow bill with overlapping red and black spots.

GREAT BLACK-BACKED GULL *Larus marinus.* 29" (74 cm). A huge gull with a jet-black mantle. First-winter immature is pale brownish with a darker, "checkered" mantle, suggesting the adult pattern. Older immatures gradually acquire adult plumage over four years. At all ages, note the massive bill. Fierce and powerful, this species steals food from other gulls, scavenges on carrion and garbage, and preys on eggs and young in seabird colonies. Its North Atlantic coastal range is expanding southward, and westward into the Great Lakes.

LARGER GULLS

winter adult

Herring

first-winter

second-winter

first-winter

Great Black-backed

first-winter

winter adult

Ring-billed

GREAT BLACK-BACKED GULL

first-winter immature

HERRING GULL

breeding

breeding

RING-BILLED GULL

first-winter immature

BLACK-LEGGED KITTIWAKE *Rissa tridactyla*. 17"
(43 cm). Small gull of the open ocean and seacoasts.
Strictly a winter visitor along the North Atlantic coast;
mostly offshore but rarely ventures into harbors and
inlets. Identified by its slim, unmarked yellow bill, cool
gray mantle that pales to silver on the outer flight feathers, and solid black wing tips. Adult in winter plumage
has a dusky smudge on the nape. Immature flashes a
bold pattern of black and white on the wings, similar to
that of the much smaller immature Bonaparte's Gull, but
young Kittiwake has an additional black collar across
the nape.

BONAPARTE'S GULL *Larus philadelphia*. 13½" (34 cm).
Small, "hooded" gull with flashy white wedges on its
outer wings. In winter, slender, white-headed adult
with dark ear mark seems ternlike, but note the square
tail and short, delicate bill. Immature is distinguished
from other common gulls by small size, boldly patterned wings, and grayish ear spot. Widespread
migrant; in winter gathers in large flocks on coastal
waters, larger rivers, and the Great Lakes.

FRANKLIN'S GULL *Larus pipixcan*. 14" (37 cm). The
common, black-headed gull of the Great Plains; rare on
the Atlantic coast. Nests on prairie marshes but also forages on farmland; feeds mostly on insects, often hawking them in the air. Adult is distinguished from the
slightly larger Laughing Gull (with which it may be
seen during migration along the Texas coast) by the narrow white area separating the gray wings from the black
and white wing tips; immature and winter-plumage
Franklin's Gulls have darker head patches and more
prominent white eye rings. The smaller Bonaparte's
flashes much more white in the wings.

LAUGHING GULL *Larus atricilla*. 16½" (42 cm). Slender,
black-headed gull of the Atlantic and Gulf coasts; named
for its laughlike calls. Adults are "hooded" only in
spring and early summer; at other times they have
grayish smudges on the backs of their heads. Mantle is
darker gray than that of other small Eastern gulls. The
wing tips are black. Juveniles, usually seen with adults
in late summer, are dusky brown with light bellies.
Older immatures resemble winter adults but have
brown-tinged wings and dark tail bands. Very common
on beaches, salt marshes, and estuaries.

Black-Legged
Kittiwake

immature

Bonaparte's

nonbreeding

nonbreeding

Franklin's

Laughing

winter
adult

nonbreeding

breeding

BONAPARTE'S
GULL

nonbreeding

first-winter
immature

breeding

FRANKLIN'S
GULL

LAUGHING
GULL

juvenile

nonbreeding

breeding

SMALLER GULLS

TERNS Sleek cousins of the gulls and skimmers, these graceful water birds are swift and powerful in flight. They have long pointed wings, forked tails, and daggerlike bills. They feed by diving headfirst into the water to catch small fish. Terns typically nest in noisy colonies on beaches, sandbars, dunes, or marshes. They will fiercely defend their territories, often fearlessly dive-bombing unwary beach strollers.

BLACK TERN *Chlidonias niger*. 10" (25 cm). Small, dark tern of freshwater marshes and lakes. Black-bodied breeding adult is unmistakable. Nonbreeding adult, as well as immature, is darker above than other terns, with a dusky helmet-shaped head patch, a distinctive smudge on the sides of the breast, and a short gray tail. The Black Tern hawks insects in flight, darting gracefully, like an oversized swallow, low over marshes. Uncommon and declining breeder inland; uncommon but regular migrant on coastal marshes. Winters in South America.

LEAST TERN *Sterna antillarum*. 9" (23 cm). Tiny, slender, and silvery gray, with a yellow bill and white forehead; much smaller than other pale-backed terns. Seems hyperactive in flight, bounding on stiff, rapid wingbeats; hovers buoyantly before plunging into the surf. Nests on sandy beaches and exposed sandbars in large rivers, both seriously endangered habitats. In much of its breeding range, it has become quite rare.

FORSTER'S TERN *Sterna forsteri*. 14¾" (38 cm). Common nesting tern of inland marshes and coastal wetlands. Not easily distinguishable from Common Tern, except in fall and winter, when Forster's sports a diagnostic dark ear patch completely surrounded by white. In summer, note the silvery primaries and orange bill and legs; also listen for the Forster's low, nasal *tza-a-ap* call.

COMMON TERN *Sterna hirundo*. 14½" (37 cm). Smaller than most gulls and sleeker, with a black cap, red bill, and long forked tail. A common summer resident of coastal beaches and northern lakes; also a widespread migrant. Winters primarily south of the U.S. Immatures and nonbreeding adults have pale foreheads, dark bills, and a dusky bar on their shoulders. Familiar call is a harsh, grating *kee-ar-r*. The very similar **Roseate Tern** is an uncommon summer visitor along the outer North Atlantic coast. Roseates are seabirds, rarely seen except near breeding colonies, and are difficult to distinguish from Common Terns.

SMALLER TERNS

on nest

breeding

nonbreeding

BLACK TERN

breeding

Common

breeding

breeding

Forster's

LEAST TERN

Least
breeding

breeding

FORSTER'S
TERN

nonbreeding

first-winter
immature

COMMON
TERN

breeding

GULL-BILLED TERN *Sterna nilotica*. 14½" (37 cm). Pale tern of southern beaches, salt marshes, bays, and inlets. Quite gull-like; note the stout black bill and shallow, forked tail. Feeds mostly on insects, which it hawks in flight. Ranges as far north as Long Island, New York (sparingly), in summer; limited to Florida and the Gulf Coast in winter. In the fall its black cap is replaced by a dusky nape and small ear patch, less extensive than the comparable pattern on the head of the sleeker Forster's Tern (p. 78).

ROYAL TERN *Sterna maxima*. 19½" (50 cm). A large tern of the Atlantic and Gulf coasts, with a stout orange beak and shaggy crest. Its black cap, worn only during spring courtship, molts into nonbreeding plumage with white forehead by midsummer, while the birds are still nesting. Breeds in large colonies on sandy barrier islands, locally north to Maryland; in late summer may disperse as far north as Massachusetts. Very common winter resident of southern beaches, south of the Carolinas. Frequently seen patrolling just beyond the breakers, diving into the surf from great heights. The **Sandwich Tern**, a slender, crested tern of southern coasts, has a similar plumage sequence, but its bill is thin and black, with a distinctive yellow tip. Compare with the similarly sized Gull-billed Tern.

CASPIAN TERN *Sterna caspia*. 21" (54 cm). Our largest tern; gull-sized, with a massive blood-red bill. This is the only large tern likely to be seen inland. Nests at widely scattered sites on marshes, rivers, and lakeshores; also locally along the coast. Compared to the Royal Tern, the Caspian has a thicker, redder bill, less deeply forked tail, dark undersides of the outer wings, and a black or streaked grayish forehead (never white, as in nonbreeding Royal).

BLACK SKIMMER *Rynchops niger*. 18" (46 cm). Striking ternlike resident of coastal waters; distinguished by black and white plumage and unique bicolored bill, with lower mandible longer than the upper. Young are mottled brownish above (p. 17). Buoyant and leisurely in flight, it flies low, often in small, noisy flocks, just skimming the water, lower mandible slicing the surface and snapping shut on small fish. Nests in colonies with gulls and terns on sandy barrier beaches.

Caspian
nonbreeding

Royal
nonbreeding

Gull-billed
nonbreeding

breeding

Skimmer

GULL-BILLED
TERN

breeding

SANDWICH
TERN

nonbreeding

nonbreeding

ROYAL TERN

breeding

CASPIAN TERN

breeding

breeding

BLACK SKIMMER

LARGER TERNS AND SKIMMER

PIGEONS AND DOVES This is a widespread family, typified by the ordinary city pigeon. Its full breast, small round head, and stubby legs, as well as its swift, powerful flight and familiar head-bobbing strut, are common to most members of the family. In general, the distinction between pigeons and doves is one of size; the smaller species are known as doves. Some Asian and Pacific species rank among the world's most spectacularly colorful birds, though in America most are cloaked in drab earth tones, splashed on the neck with just a small slick of iridescence. They forage on the ground, feeding mostly on seeds, and are common visitors to backyard feeders, barnyards, and city parks.

ROCK DOVE (DOMESTIC PIGEON) *Columba livia.* 13¼" (34 cm). Native to Europe, where the ancestral population still inhabits coastal cliffs and mountain crags. Today, skyscraper ledges, barn rafters, or highway abutments substitute for its native habitat. Centuries of domestication have generated an extremely variable plumage, from pure white to solid black or rust-colored, although the original and most common form is gray with a white rump and dark tail band and wing bars. No other gray pigeon is found in the East, except in extreme southern Florida, where the **White-crowned Pigeon** can be told by its uniform blackish-slate plumage and white cap.

MOURNING DOVE *Zenaida macroura.* 12" (31 cm). Slender and delicate; warm tan in color, with a long, pointed tail that flashes white on the sides. Our most common native dove. Inhabits city parks, suburbs, roadsides, farmland, and other open country. Its muted call, a repetitive *ohh? hoo, hoo, hoo,* is often mistaken for an owl's. In flight, its wings make a soft whistling sound. The **White-winged Dove** of southern Texas and, rarely, the Gulf Coast, is similar in size and color but with a squared tail and bold white wing patches. It prefers more arid country with scattered brush.

COMMON GROUND-DOVE *Columbina passerina.* 6¾" (17 cm). Tiny sparrow-sized dove, with a short, squared dark tail and bright reddish-brown primaries. Locally common but declining resident of gardens, farmyards, brushy roadsides, and other open country. Most often seen when flushed from the ground. In central and southern Texas, the **Inca Dove**, which inhabits similar but more arid habitats, also flashes reddish in the wings, but tail is longer and bordered with white. Dark edges on the feathers give its plumage a scaly appearance.

Common
Ground-Dove

Inca Dove

Mourning
Doves

Rock Doves

White-winged
Dove

White-crowned
Pigeon

ROCK DOVE
(Domestic Pigeon)

MOURNING
DOVE

COMMON
GROUND-DOVE

INCA DOVE

CUCKOOS AND ALLIES A diverse and widespread family, cuckoos and allies are represented in North America by the reclusive, woodland-dwelling cuckoos, the large terrestrial Roadrunner of southwestern deserts, and the gregarious anis, which are common residents of Central and South America that just barely range north into our area. The familiar *cuc-koo* call for which the family is named is the voice of the Common Cuckoo of the Old World.

YELLOW-BILLED CUCKOO *Coccyzus americanus.* 12" (31 cm). Slim, dove-sized summer resident of woodlands, abandoned orchards, and forest edges. Remarkably inconspicuous as it moves stealthily within the shade of dense foliage. Often heard but infrequently seen; its typical call is a rapid guttural *kukukukukukukuku kow kow kowlp kowlp*, slowing at the end. Told from the similar Black-billed Cuckoo by the yellow lower half of its beak, rusty wing flashes, and bold black and white pattern of its undertail surface.

BLACK-BILLED CUCKOO *Coccyzus erythropthalmus.* 12" (31 cm). Similar to the Yellow-billed in appearance and sluggish behavior; distinguished by its dark beak, indistinctly patterned undertail, and lack of rust color in the wings. Up close, note the narrow red eye ring (yellowish on young birds). Typical call is a monotonous series of muffled, throaty notes, given in threes or fours: *kukuku kukuku kukukuku*, etc. In the far northern states, this is the more common nesting cuckoo; farther south the Yellow-billed predominates, though either may be seen during migration.

SMOOTH-BILLED ANI *Crotophaga ani.* 13½" (34 cm). Glossy black long-tailed birds of open brush and farmland, anis could be confused only with grackles (p. 136), but the high arch of their bills gives them a unique profile. Fairly common resident of southern Florida. The nearly identical **Groove-billed Ani** is a fairly common summer resident of south Texas. The ranges of the two anis do not overlap in North America.

GREATER ROADRUNNER *Geococcyx californianus.* 22½" (32 cm). Unmistakable; large, ground-dwelling cuckoo of open scrubland and desert. Often looks disheveled, with a ragged crest and a long tail cocked at odd angles. Seldom flies but can run at amazing speeds, its neck straining forward and tail trailing as a counterweight. With speed, agility, and a formidable beak, the Roadrunner preys on insects, lizards, snakes, small rodents, and other birds.

CUCKOOS AND ALLIES

BLACK-BILLED
CUCKOO

Black-billed

Yellow-billed

YELLOW-BILLED
CUCKOO

SMOOTH-BILLED
ANI

portrait with
crest raised
(to show scale)

GREATER
ROADRUNNER

OWLS are the nocturnal equivalents of the raptors, superbly adapted for hunting at night. Stockier in build than hawks, owls have broad heads; large eyes that face forward (for maximum light gathering and depth perception); short, bull necks; and broad, silent wings. Studies have shown that their facial disks help to gather and focus sound. Most owls spend daylight hours perched quietly in dense vegetation or tree hollows and are extremely hard to find. A regular roost may be revealed by "pellets" (regurgitated wads of indigestible hair and bone) on the ground beneath the tree, or by a noisy flock of birds harassing an owl they've discovered.

GREAT HORNED OWL *Bubo virginianus*. 22" (56 cm). Large and powerful enough to tackle jackrabbits, skunks, stray cats, and other owls. Note the prominent "ear" tufts, white chin, and finely barred belly. Our most widespread and frequently seen owl; prefers mixed woodlands near open fields but may turn up almost anywhere. Call is a series of deep, resonant hoots: *hoo hoohoo hoo hoo*. The smaller and much slimmer Long-eared Owl (p. 88) has closely spaced "ears" and vertical streaks on its belly.

SNOWY OWL *Nyctea scandiaca*. 24" (61 cm). Large and snowy white; variably barred and spotted with black (much more so in females and young). This rare winter visitor from the Arctic periodically invades the northern states, keeping to open-country habitats similar to its native tundra, especially coastal dunes, farmland, airports, and landfills. Fairly active during daylight.

BARRED OWL *Strix varia*. 20½" (53 cm). Large dark-eyed owl with a boldly barred breast and streaked belly; lacks "ear" tufts. Common in moist deciduous forests, wooded swamps, and bottomlands, especially in the deep South. In winter it may wander into city parks and suburbs. Most active at night, and more often heard than seen; typical call is a rhythmic series of barks ending with a distinctive drawl: *hoo hoo hoohoo, hoo hoo hoohoo-awww*.

BARN OWL *Tyto alba*. 16½" (43 cm). Slender, ghostly pale resident of belfries, barns, and grain silos; also adapts to nest boxes and abandoned buildings in and near cities. Hunts in open areas. Appears deceptively large, especially in flight, due to oversized wings and long legs. Primarily nocturnal, Barn Owls can nab a mouse or rat in pitch-darkness, relying solely on their acute hearing.

LARGER OWLS

male

GREAT HORNED
OWL

SNOWY OWL

female

BARRED OWL

BARN OWL

SHORT-EARED OWL *Asio flammeus*. 15" (39 cm). Crow-sized owl of marshes, dunes, prairies, and open country; formerly widespread, now quite local. Most active at dawn and dusk; often seen perched on a fence-post or flapping buoyantly low over the ground. The Short-eared's tiny "ears" are barely noticeable. On flying birds, the best marks are the pale ochre wing patches; or from below, the dark crescents on the wrists. (Compare to Northern Harrier, p. 46, and Rough-legged Hawk, p. 48, which frequent similar habitats.) The related **Long-eared Owl** is a nocturnal and rarely seen resident of dense woods. Its conspicuous "ears" and rusty face are suggestive of the much huskier Great Horned Owl (p. 86). Both Short-eared Owls and Long-eared Owls are somewhat migratory and in winter may gather in small groups, roosting in thickets or dense conifer groves.

EASTERN SCREECH-OWL *Otus asio*. 9" (23 cm). Common, small, "eared" owl of suburbs, orchards, parks, and open woodlands, but rarely seen. Roosts by day in old woodpecker holes or hollow stumps, or tucked up tight against a tree trunk, perfectly camouflaged. In most regions the red and gray color morphs occur with similar frequency. Typical call is not a screech but a quavering whistle, on one pitch or descending. Screech-Owls will sometimes respond to an imitation of their call, as will flocks of small birds, which gather around the impostor, seemingly eager to mob the nearby "owl."

NORTHERN SAW-WHET OWL *Aegolius acadicus*. 8" (18 cm). Smallest owl in the East; distinguished by its squat body and rounded head. Breeds deep in moist northern coniferous forests. In winter it is most often observed roosting in dense evergreen shrubs in parks, cemeteries, and open woods. Strictly nocturnal, Saw-whets are, by day, remarkably tame but should not be disturbed.

BURROWING OWL *Speotyto cunicularia*. 9¼" (24 cm). Small, diurnal (active by day) owl of open country, including prairies, rangeland, even airports. Note its rounded head and barred breast. Young birds are unmarked buff below. Burrowing owls nest underground, mostly in old prairie dog tunnels or other animal burrows, but they can also excavate their own nest holes. May sometimes nest in small colonies. Typically seen perched erect on their long legs, atop a mound of dirt by their nest or on a low shrub or fence post.

SMALLER OWLS

SHORT-EARED
OWL

LONG-EARED
OWL

gray morph

NORTHERN
SAW-WHET OWL

EASTERN
SCREECH-OWL

red morph

BURROWING
OWL

juvenile

CHIMNEY SWIFT *Chaetura pelagica.* 5¼" (14 cm). A small sooty-gray aerial gymnast; seems hyperactive as it darts and glides about on stiffly fluttering wings, snatching airborne insects. Note the blunt tail and long, narrow wings that appear to arc back from the body without a bend—a distinctive shape that distinguishes swifts from swallows (p. 102). Common in towns and cities; congregates in large colonies that chip and twitter loudly overhead. Chimney Swifts roost and nest inside chimneys or hollow tree stumps, where they cling to the vertical walls with tiny feet and stiff bristles on the tips of their tails. They rarely, if ever, perch elsewhere.

NIGHTJARS, also known as Goatsuckers, are the peerless insect eaters of the night. Well camouflaged, most roost inconspicuously on the ground or perched lengthwise along a tree limb by day, then take to the skies at dusk, snatching insects in their incredibly wide mouths. On many species, a net of fine, bristlelike feathers surrounds the beak, in effect making it even wider. Due to their nocturnal habits, most nightjars are seldom seen and are best known by their distinctive and familiar calls. Nighthawks, however, may be active at any hour, especially twilight. They are told from other nightjars by their long, pointed wings, which, on perched birds, reach to the tips of their tails.

COMMON NIGHTHAWK *Chordeiles minor.* 9½" (24 cm). Dark, slender, long-winged; bounds buoyantly and erratically with each deliberate flap of its angular wings. In good light, look for the white slash across each wing; male also has a white throat and a narrow white tail band. Often hunts in small groups, calling through the night; voice a nasal, insectlike *beeent.* Fairly common but declining summer resident throughout the East, especially over cities and towns, where it nests on flat, graveled rooftops.

WHIP-POOR-WILL *Camprimulgus vociferus.* 9½" (24 cm). Although its distinctive *whip-po-weeo* call, tirelessly repeated for hours, is a familiar sound of late-spring and summer nights, the Whip-poor-will is seldom seen. Its mottled, brownish plumage blends perfectly with the leaf litter in which it quietly rests during the day. When flushed, the rounded brownish wings and flashy white tail corners (buff on females) identify it. In southern states the larger **Chuck-will's-widow** also calls its name repeatedly throughout the night: a quick, four-syllabled *ch'k-wills-w'dow.*

SWIFT AND NIGHTJARS

Swifts

Nighthawk

CHIMNEY SWIFT

COMMON NIGHTHAWK

male

female

CHUCK-WILL'S-WIDOW

male

WHIP-POOR-WILL

RUBY-THROATED HUMMINGBIRD *Archilochus colubris.* 3½" (9 cm). Our tiniest bird; a glittering jewel of iridescent green and ruby-red, renowned for its hovering, insectlike flight. Fairly common summer resident of woodlands, clearings, and rural gardens. Tame and inquisitive, it buzzes from flower to flower, probing with its needlelike bill for energy-rich nectar. Studies show that hummingbirds perceive red colors the best and show a clear preference for red or orange tubular flowers, though they will readily visit feeders offering plain sugar water. The Ruby-throat is the only regularly occurring hummingbird of the East. Stray hummingbirds observed along the Gulf Coast in winter are more likely to belong to one of our numerous Western species.

BELTED KINGFISHER *Ceryle alcyon.* 13" (33 cm). Common resident of ponds, streams, rivers, and coastal waters. Immediately recognized by its top-heavy profile, diving behavior, and loud, grating rattle. Often perches on an exposed waterside snag or pier, from which it may dive directly, or else it hovers above the surface before plunging down to snatch a fish, a frog, or perhaps a crayfish. In flight, flashes small white wing patches. Note that the female is marked with an additional brownish "belt" across her belly. Kingfishers nest in burrows tunneled into an exposed riverbank or sand pit.

WOODPECKERS are expert tree climbers. Grasping with strong claws and propped up by stiff tail feathers, they hitch themselves up tree trunks and use their sturdy, chisel-like beaks to probe, hack, or drill for insects. Woodpeckers dig nest holes in standing tree trunks and limbs (usually in dead or dying wood). These holes are used in subsequent years by other cavity-nesting species. Most species share a distinctive undulating style of flight—rising with a few quick flaps and then dipping as the wings are briefly tucked closed. Characteristic rump and wing patches are most evident in flight. Many species also have loud calls, which are worth learning, as woodpeckers are often heard long before they are spotted.

PILEATED WOODPECKER *Dryocopus pileatus.* 17" (44 cm). Unmistakable crow-sized woodpecker. Mostly black with a flaming red crest and white flashes in the wings. Resident of mature forests, older second growth, and occasionally wooded suburbs. The Pileated is shy and surprisingly inconspicuous. Its presence is often indicated only by the elongated holes and troughs it has hewn into tree trunks. Most common in the South.

RUBY-THROATED
HUMMINGBIRD

male

female

BELTED
KINGFISHER

male

female

plunge diving

PILEATED
WOODPECKER

male

male

female

NORTHERN FLICKER *Colaptes auratus.* 12½" (32 cm) Atypical; large brownish woodpecker that often forages on the ground for ants and grubs. Note the barred upperparts, black crescent across the chest, red patch on the nape, and (on males) the black whisker marks. In flight, the flashy yellow undersides of the wings and white rump are unmistakable. Common in open country, parks, suburbs, forest edges, and along roadsides. The eastern subspecies is "yellow-shafted," but west of the Rockies, Flickers are "red-shafted," having salmon-pink wing linings and red whiskers. Red-shafted birds and hybrids of the two subspecies may be seen east into the Great Plains. Flickers are highly vocal; common calls include a loud, ringing *wick, wick, wick, wick, wick, wick;* a quieter, almost squeaky *flicka, flicka, flicka;* and a single-note *klee-yer.*

RED-BELLIED WOODPECKER *Melanerpes carolinus.* 9½" (24 cm). Striking; barred black and white above, grayish buff below, with a brilliant red cap (on females, only the nape is red). Its white rump and small white wing patches are conspicuous only in flight. The red-tinged belly feathers are difficult to see. A familiar and noisy resident of suburbs, parks, open woodlands, pinewoods, and swampy bottomland forests, especially in the South. In recent years this species has been extending its range northward into New England and has become a regular visitor at winter feeding stations. Most common call is a loud, rolling *churr.* In drier habitats of central and southern Texas, the Red-bellied is replaced by the very similar **Golden-fronted Woodpecker**. Males are distinguished by their multi-colored head patches. Females resemble female Red-bellieds but have golden napes.

RED-HEADED WOODPECKER *Melanerpes erythro-cephalus.* 9½" (24 cm). Adults are unmistakable; juveniles have dull brownish heads but are readily told by their white rumps and wing patches. (Compare the shape and location of the wing patches to those on young sapsuckers, p. 96.) In the Midwest and South, a locally common and conspicuous resident of parks, open country with scattered trees, and pine and oak woodlands. Typically perches high on a dead limb, calling loudly and occasionally sallying forth, flycatcherlike, to snatch insects on the wing. Among its several calls is a harsh, rolling *queark* similar to the Red-bellied's. Red-headeds have become quite rare in the Northeast.

WOODPECKERS II

Red-headed

Flickers

male

female in nest hole

"Yellow-shafted"

NORTHERN FLICKER

"Red-shafted"

Red-bellied

male

RED-BELLIED WOODPECKER

female

juvenile

RED-HEADED WOODPECKER

GOLDEN-FRONTED WOODPECKER

male

DOWNY WOODPECKER *Picoides pubescens.* 6½" (1 cm). Very small black and white woodpecker with an unmarked white back and a short, stubby bill. Our tamest and most familiar woodpecker, the Downy nests in woodlands, in suburban backyards, and even in city parks, and readily visits feeders during winter. It often travels with mixed flocks of small songbirds, foraging on reed stalks or among the small outer branches of a tree, clinging upside down like a chickadee. Its calls include a sharp *pik* and a staccato "whinny," descending in pitch at the end. In dry scrub and mesquite of Texas and Oklahoma, the Downy is replaced by the slightly larger **Ladder-backed Woodpecker**.

HAIRY WOODPECKER *Picoides villosus.* 9½" (23 cm). Nearly identical to the Downy but larger, with a proportionately longer beak and unmarked white outer tail feathers (these are barred on the Downy). Fairly common in forests and woodlots, the Hairy is shyer than the Downy and less frequently seen near houses, although it will visit suet feeders. Call is a sharp *peek,* louder and more emphatic than the Downy's note. In coniferous forests of the far North, Hairys might be confused with the uncommon and reclusive **Black-backed** or **Three-toed Woodpeckers**. The Black-backed occurs farther south and is more likely to be seen by most birders. It appears much darker than the Hairy, with dense barring on the sides, a black back, and (on males) a yellow crown. The Black-backed forages almost exclusively by chipping the bark off dead trees in spruce bogs, burnt-over areas, and flooded stands of timber.

YELLOW-BELLIED SAPSUCKER *Sphyrapicus varius.* 8½" (22 cm). Vertical white wing stripe is diagnostic in all plumages. Also note black chest mark, mottled back, red forehead, and (on males) red throat. In flight, the wing stripe and white rump are conspicuous. Juveniles are variably mottled and brownish but usually suggest adult pattern. They retain this plumage through much of their first winter (compare to the species on p. 94). Sapsuckers drill rows of holes into live trees and feed on both the oozing sap and the insects that are attracted to it. These unique horizontal lines of holes (look for them on fruit trees, aspens, and birches) are often the best indication of the sapsuckers' presence, as the birds are typically shy and reclusive. Their call, a hesitant nasal *kee-eerr,* is heard primarily on the breeding grounds.

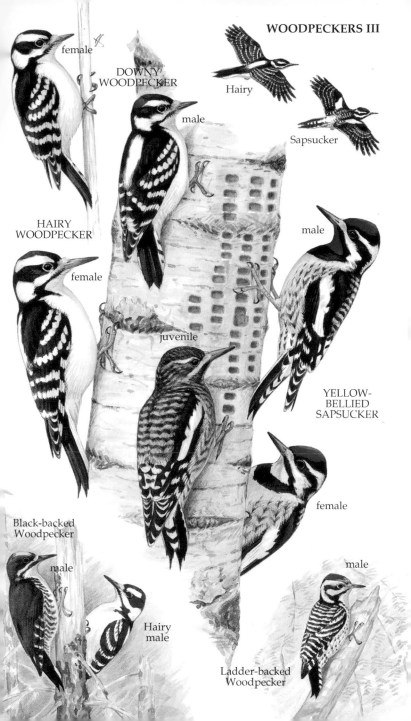

female

DOWNY
WOODPECKER

male

Hairy

Sapsucker

HAIRY
WOODPECKER

female

male

juvenile

YELLOW-
BELLIED
SAPSUCKER

female

Black-backed
Woodpecker

male

Hairy
male

male

Ladder-backed
Woodpecker

FLYCATCHERS Slender perching birds, flycatchers have a slightly crested, angular profile, an upright posture, and a characteristic aerial foraging behavior. They sit patiently on an exposed perch, darting out every so often to snatch passing insects. In this highly migratory family, most North American species winter in the tropics and return north as insects appear in the spring. The kingbirds, conspicuous inhabitants of open country, are known for their pugnacious behavior and often harass crows or large hawks. The small, drab species discussed on p. 100 are much less noticeable and are often difficult to identify. Listen carefully for a song or call note; note the shape and color of the beak and other field marks, such as an eye ring or wing bars; look also for behavioral twitches, such as tail pumping or wing flicking.

EASTERN KINGBIRD *Tyrannus tyrannus.* 8½" (22 cm). Trim slate, black, and white plumage, with an ample tail that flashes a white band across the tip. The red crown patch is nearly always concealed. Common near farms and roadsides, and in parks, streamside thickets, and open country with scattered trees. Often perches on fences or telephone lines. The **Gray Kingbird** of coastal Florida is paler than the Eastern Kingbird, with a dark "mask," large beak, and slightly forked, all-dark tail. The Gray Kingbird is a locally common summer resident, especially on the Florida Keys.

WESTERN KINGBIRD *Tyrannus verticalis.* 8½" (22 cm). Shape and behavior suggest Eastern Kingbird; pale grayish, tinged green on the back, with a lemon-yellow belly. Note the square-tipped black tail with narrow white margins. Common in the Great Plains and prairies; rare fall migrant on the East Coast.

SCISSOR-TAILED FLYCATCHER *Tyrannus forficatus.* 11" (28 cm) to 15" (38 cm). Spectacular prairie kingbird with long scissorlike tail, pinkish-buff flanks, and salmon wing linings. Often seen perched on a low shrub or fence. Young birds lack the tail streamers and can be mistaken for Western Kingbirds. Note their forked tails and buff or pinkish (not yellow) flanks.

GREAT CRESTED FLYCATCHER *Myiarchus crinitus.* 8½" (22 cm). Our largest woodland flycatcher; brownish-olive with a gray breast, yellow belly, and rusty flashes in the wings and tail. Common and noisy summer resident of mixed open woodlands, orchards, parks, and rural backyards, but feeds high among the treetops and is often hard to find. Calls include a loud, emphatic *wheeep!* and rolling *brrreeep.*

FLYCATCHERS I

EASTERN KINGBIRD

Kingbirds

Eastern

Western

WESTERN KINGBIRD

GRAY KINGBIRD

SCISSOR-TAILED FLYCATCHER

GREAT CRESTED FLYCATCHER

at nest hole

EASTERN PHOEBE *Sayornis phoebe.* 7" (18 cm). Drab olive flycatcher with a dark head and small black beak. Emphatically pumps its tail when perched. Common and widespread around farms and in semi-open country, especially near water. Typically builds its nest on a ledge under a cliff or bridge, or in a barn or deserted building. Its song is a sneezy *feebee,* repeated tirelessly. In northern states, Phoebes are among the earliest spring migrants, often arriving by late March. **Say's Phoebe** replaces the Eastern Phoebe in the dry, open habitats of the western plains. It is grayish-brown with a black tail and cinnamon belly.

EASTERN WOOD-PEWEE *Contopus virens.* 6¼" (16 cm). Small grayish-green flycatcher; resembles Eastern Phoebe but has two pale wing bars and a paler head (the same tone as its back). Its beak is noticeably wide and flattened and has an orange base. Common but inconspicuous summer resident of deciduous forests and open woodlands. Typically forages high within the forest canopy, its presence revealed only by its song, a lazy, sweet, whistled *peee-a-weee* (pause) *pee-ooo.*

OLIVE-SIDED FLYCATCHER *Contopus borealis.* 7½" (19 cm). A disproportionately large head and beak and fairly short tail distinguish this summer resident of northern bogs and coniferous forests. Note the dark olive "vest" and white stripe down the middle of its breast. Usually flycatches from a high, exposed snag. Most frequently seen as a migrant in late spring and early fall.

LEAST FLYCATCHER *Empidonax minimus.* 5¼" (13 cm). Smaller and more compact than a Wood-Pewee, with a crisp white eye ring and wing bars. Often seems agitated as it flicks its wings and tail while perched. Best identified by its song, a dry, emphatic *che-bek!* Fairly common migrant throughout the East; nests in open woodlands and orchards. The Least is the most familiar of the Eastern *Empidonax* flycatchers, a genus of small, drab flycatchers that are nearly indistinguishable by sight alone. Luckily, each has a distinct song or call by which it can be identified. The **Willow Flycatcher** is locally common in brushy margins of streams, marshes, and pastures. Slightly larger and browner than the Least, it may lack a distinct eye ring. Its song is a sneezy *fitz-bew!* The **Acadian Flycatcher**, which represents the genus in moist southeastern woodlands, sings an explosive, rising *spitzeet!*

FLYCATCHERS II

on nest

EASTERN
PHOEBE

Phoebe

EASTERN
WOOD-PEWEE

OLIVE-SIDED
FLYCATCHER

LEAST
FLYCATCHER

Empidonax
Flycatchers

WILLOW
FLYCATCHER

SWALLOWS Small and slender, swallows epitomize grace. With long, pointed wings, they swoop and glide in the sky or skim low across ponds and wetlands, snapping up small insects in their wide mouths. Swallows often perch on phone lines and wires; migrants may gather in flocks of thousands. Compare to Chimney Swift (p. 90).

TREE SWALLOW *Tachycineta bicolor*. 5¾" (15 cm). Glossy blue-green above; clean white below. Common in upland fields and around wetlands. Nests in tree cavities or nest boxes. Juvenile (seen in midsummer through fall) is brownish-gray above with a dusky wash across the breast. It may be confused with the other brown-backed species, the Bank Swallow and **Northern Rough-winged Swallow**. The Rough-winged, which has a dusky throat and breast, is locally common in open country near rivers and wetlands.

BANK SWALLOW *Riparia riparia*. 5¼" (13 cm). Small swallow with brown back and diagnostic dark breast band, which is often difficult to discern as this dynamo zips by. Fairly common migrant; nests locally in colonies burrowed into riverbanks, road cuts, and excavations.

CLIFF SWALLOW *Hirundo pyrrhonota*. 5¾" (15 cm). Dark back and rusty throat suggest Barn Swallow, but square tail, pale tawny rump, and creamy forehead are unique. Locally common in rural areas, especially west of the Mississippi. Nests in large colonies, its gourd-shaped nests of mud often clustered under cliffs, highway abutments, or building eaves.

BARN SWALLOW *Hirundo rustica*. 6¾" (18 cm). Our most familiar swallow. Glossy bluish-black above, buff or rusty below, with a long, slender, deeply forked tail (shorter on juveniles). A common migrant and summer resident of open spaces, especially around farms and homesteads. Barn Swallows plaster their cupped nests of mud and grass onto the joists of barns and other open structures.

PURPLE MARTIN *Progne subis*. 8" (20 cm). Large, starling-sized swallow. Male often appears black; note its soaring flight and forked tail. Seen from above, female has a narrow grayish collar. Common and wide-spread summer resident of the South; uncommon and local in the North. Purple Martin prefers open country near water. Native Americans first attracted colonies of mosquito-devouring Martins to nest in clusters of hollowed gourds. Today they nest almost exclusively in manufactured "apartment" birdhouses.

SWALLOWS

Tree

Bank

Cliff

juvenile

Rough-winged

TREE SWALLOW

juvenile

BANK
SWALLOW

CLIFF
SWALLOW

BARN
SWALLOW

female

PURPLE
MARTIN

male

martin
house

Barn Swallow

juvenile

CROWS AND JAYS These birds are renowned for their resourcefulness. They learn quickly to exploit new food sources around human settlements and disturbed habitats. Crows, magpies, and ravens scavenge on roadside carrion and in landfills and grainfields. The rambunctious jays often forage around picnic grounds and campsites and are familiar visitors to backyard feeders. Most species have a varied repertoire of harsh, raucous calls.

BLUE JAY *Cyanocitta cristata.* 11½" (29 cm). Familiar crested jay of the East. Note the broad white wing bars and white tips of the tail feathers. Common and conspicuous resident of deciduous forests, wooded parks, and suburbs throughout the East. Typically forages in pairs or small groups that noisily call to one another. While nesting, however, Blue Jays are shy and surprisingly quiet. The **Scrub Jay**, a local and uncommon resident in the oak scrub of central Florida, has no crest, and its blue wings and tail are unmarked.

GRAY JAY *Perisoreus canadensis.* 11¾" (30 cm). Formerly known as Canada Jay. This uncrested gray and white jay of northern coniferous forests is a bold and inquisitive visitor to campsites and cabins. Juveniles are dark gray.

AMERICAN CROW *Corvus brachyrhynchos.* 18½" (48 cm). Well-known and abundant resident of semi-open country and farmland throughout the East. Congregates in nonbreeding season into large, noisy flocks that are often seen mobbing large hawks or owls. A second species, the **Fish Crow**, is locally common south of New England near beaches and coastal marshes, and along estuaries and larger rivers; nests also in the Mississippi Valley. Slightly smaller than the American Crow, it is best identified by its call, a higher-pitched, nasal *cuh* or two-syllabled *cah-uh,* quite distinct from the throaty *caw* of the American Crow.

COMMON RAVEN *Corvus corax.* 24" (62 cm). Large, crowlike resident of mountainous terrain and coniferous forests. Uncommon; distinguished from the crow by its large size; massive beak; long, wedge-shaped tail; and soaring, hawklike flight. Call is a deep *croak.*

BLACK-BILLED MAGPIE *Pica pica.* 19" (49 cm). Flashy, unmistakable resident of the western plains. Locally common resident of streamside thickets and woodlands and around ranches and farms. Usually seen in small flocks. Quite noisy, its calls include raspy whining notes and a series of harsh, querulous *crecks.*

CROWS AND JAYS

BLUE JAY

Scrub Jay

GRAY JAY

Raven

Crow

BLACK-BILLED MAGPIES

COMMON RAVEN

AMERICAN CROW

TITMICE A widely distributed family, titmice are small, active mostly grayish woodland birds. In North America, species with crests are called titmice, while those having fluffy rounded crowns and dark caps and bibs are referred to as chickadees. Familiar residents of parks and suburban backyards, chickadees and titmice are remarkably tame. They are often the first to come to a newly stocked feeder; with patience, they may be coaxed to take sunflower seeds from the hand. They also readily respond to "spishing" noises or imitations of owl calls and may approach to within a few feet of the caller. Except when nesting, they are highly social and travel in family groups or mixed flocks with other small birds. Quick and acrobatic, titmice often cling upside down as they use their small bills to probe twigs, bark, and dried weeds for insect eggs and pupae. They are cavity nesters and often use old woodpecker holes.

BLACK-CAPPED CHICKADEE *Parus atricapillus*. 5¼" (13 cm). Common chickadee of the northern states; known by its black crown and bib and familiar *tsick-a-dee* call. Also sings a clear, whistled, descending *fee bee*. Resident of woodlands, parks, and wooded suburbs; also thickets in winter. Along the southern margin of its range, this species can be extremely difficult to distinguish from the Carolina Chickadee, with which it may hybridize. In dense coniferous forests of the far North, listen for the lazy *tseek-a-day-day* call of the **Boreal Chickadee**. If it can be "spished" into the open, note its dingy brownish back and cap and brown flanks.

CAROLINA CHICKADEE *Parus carolinensis*. 4¾" (12 cm). Small chickadee of the Southeast; closely related to, and often indistinguishable from, its northern sibling where their ranges overlap. It is slightly smaller and shorter-tailed than the Black-capped and lacks white edges on its greater wing coverts (on the front half of the folded wing) and secondaries. The Carolina's *tsick-a-dee* call is more hurried than the Black-capped's; its 3- or 4-note song, *fee bee see bay*, is higher-pitched.

TUFTED TITMOUSE *Parus bicolor*. 6¼" (16 cm). Small, crested lead-gray songbird with peach-colored flanks. Typical adult has a black forehead; "black-crested" subspecies of central Texas has a pale forehead and black crest. Common in deciduous woodlands, parks, and backyards. Its most distinctive song is a sweet, whistled, *peter, peter,* etc. Has extended its range northward in recent years.

BOREAL
CHICKADEE

TITMICE

BLACK-CAPPED
CHICKADEE

CAROLINA
CHICKADEE

"Black-crested"
subspecies
(Texas)

TUFTED
TITMOUSE

NUTHATCHES These small, stocky, short-tailed forest dwellers forage while clinging to tree trunks and limbs and characteristically work their way down a trunk headfirst. With a slender, sharply pointed beak that appears slightly upturned, they hack and probe into crevices in search of seeds, insect eggs, and pupae. Nuthatches commonly associate with mixed flocks of titmice, creepers, kinglets, and woodpeckers. Although they tend to retire into the depths of the forest while nesting, during winter they may become quite tame around feeding stations offering suet or sunflower seeds.

WHITE-BREASTED NUTHATCH *Sitta carolinensis*. 5¾" (15 cm). Blue-gray above, white below, with white flashes in the tail and a white face clearly punctuated by a dark eye. Male has a glossy black crown that is duller and grayer on the female. Widespread and familiar resident of parks, suburbs, and deciduous forests. Unlike smaller nuthatches, it forages almost exclusively along trunks and major tree limbs, shunning the outer branches. Call is distinctive: a nasal *ya ya ya ya*.

RED-BREASTED NUTHATCH *Sitta canadensis*. 4½" (11 cm). Small nuthatch of northern coniferous forests and higher elevations in the Appalachian mountains. Distinguished by its black eye line, narrow white eyebrow, and cinnamon underparts (paler on females). Active and highly vocal. Typically forages in conifers, often among the outer boughs, where it pries seeds from the cones. Its calls include a high-pitched, nasal *ank ank ank* (higher and thinner than White-breasted's). Somewhat migratory and more widespread in winter. The southern limits of its winter range may vary from year to year.

BROWN-HEADED NUTHATCH *Sitta pusilla*. 4½" (11 cm). Small nuthatch restricted to pinewoods of the southeastern states. Note dark brown cap that extends down through eye. Fairly common in appropriate habitat. Call is quite different from that of other nuthatches: a series of sharp, high-pitched squeaks and pips.

BROWN CREEPER *Certhia americana*. 5¼" (14 cm). A fairly common, though frequently overlooked, resident of mixed forests and woodlots. The exquisitely camouflaged Creeper also forages on tree trunks, but, unlike a nuthatch, it spirals upward. Note its slender, curved bill and the stiff, spiny tail feathers used as a prop as it clings tightly to the bark. Call note is a high, sibilant *seee*, its song a pair of thin, descending triplets.

NUTHATCHES AND CREEPER

female

WHITE-BREASTED
NUTHATCH

male

RED-BREASTED
NUTHATCH

female

male

BROWN-HEADED
NUTHATCH

sexes alike

BROWN
CREEPER

sexes alike

WRENS Small brownish songbirds with hunched, forward-leaning posture, expressive tails that are often cocked upward over their backs, and thin, slightly curved beaks, wrens often forage just above the ground in brush, dense tangles, and marshy areas. Their presence is revealed only by their harsh, scolding calls and loud, exuberant songs. Male wrens are energetic nest builders and may defend several nests at once. House and Carolina Wrens, familiar residents around yards and gardens, will tuck a nest almost anywhere: in a birdhouse, a drain spout, a woodpile, or even an unused mailbox.

HOUSE WREN *Troglodytes aedon.* 4¾" (12 cm). Familiar drab grayish-brown wren; widespread in gardens, orchards, brushy thickets, and open woods. Bold, excitable, and highly vocal; repeats its loud, bubbling song tirelessly through spring and summer. May be confused with the tiny, reclusive **Winter Wren**, which is darker and browner and has a stubby tail and heavy barring on the flanks. Winter Wrens creep mouselike through dense, moist undergrowth, upturned roots, and brush. They nest in coniferous or mixed forests of the North and the Appalachian highlands but are more widespread in winter.

BEWICK'S WREN *Thryomanes bewickii.* 5¼" (13 cm). Brown above, dirty white below, with a crisp white eyebrow and a long tail that it wags, cocks, and flicks, flashing its white corners. Uncommon resident of farmyards and gardens; dry scrub and open dry woodlands; declining in the Midwest.

CAROLINA WREN *Thryothorus ludovicianus.* 5½" (14 cm). Rusty upperparts, cinnamon belly, and prominent white eyebrow distinguish this common wren of the Southeast. Prefers moist thickets, open woods, and suburban yards. Distinctive song is a clear, ringing *wheedle, wheedle* or *jeh-heeva, jeh-heeva.* Periodically extends its range northward; may survive winters by visiting bird feeders.

MARSH WREN *Cistothorus palustris.* 5" (13 cm). Locally common in cattails, reeds, and rushes around freshwater and brackish marshes; the only wren that frequents this habitat. Elusive, but may perch atop an exposed stalk to belt out its explosive, bubbly song. Note white eyebrow and black-and-white-striped back. The **Sedge Wren**, told by its shorter tail, faint eyebrow, and buffy streaked crown, prefers wet sedge and grassy meadows. Fairly common in parts of the Midwest and, in winter, on the Gulf Coast. Rarely seen.

WRENS

WINTER WREN

HOUSE WREN

BEWICK'S WREN

MARSH WREN

CAROLINA WREN

MIMIC THRUSHES A New World family of slender, robin-sized songbirds with very long tails and sharp, down-curved beaks, mimic thrushes are renowned for their complex songs, which are typically a jumble of warbles, squeaks, and expertly mimicked fragments of other familiar sounds.

BROWN THRASHER *Toxostoma rufum*. 11¼" (29 cm). Bright rust above; streaked below. Plumage suggests a Wood Thrush (p. 114), but note Thrasher's slender shape, long tail, streaked (not spotted) breast, wing bars, and pale iris. Fairly common in thickets, overgrown fields, woodland edges, and gardens; local in the North. Thrashers skulk through dense, low foliage and are hard to see, but they often perch prominently to sing. They usually utter each phrase of their song twice. (Mockingbird repeats its phrases many times, Catbird rarely at all.)

GRAY CATBIRD *Dumetella carolinensis*. 8¾" (22 cm). Mouse-gray with a black cap. Long blackish tail is often cocked, revealing reddish undertail coverts. Common in gardens, thickets, woodland edges, and forest clearings. Call is a catlike whine. Song, also peppered with mewing sounds, suggests Thrasher's, but Catbird rarely repeats itself.

NORTHERN MOCKINGBIRD *Mimus polyglottos*. 10" (26 cm). Grayish with a long blackish tail and wings that flash bold white patches in flight. Conspicuous resident of southern gardens, roadsides, overgrown fields, and thickets; increasingly common in the North. Loud and persistent songster; perches high atop a tree, antenna, or phone line and often sings throughout the night. A superb mimic; each bird's song is a unique repetitive sequence of notes and phrases quoted from its avian neighbors. Call is a harsh, abrupt *tchk!*

LOGGERHEAD SHRIKE *Lanius ludovicianus*. 9" (23 cm). Cool gray above, with a black "mask," wings, and tail. In flight, white flashes in wings and tail suggest a Mockingbird, but note Shrike's distinctive bull-headed profile. Local resident of open country with scattered trees and scrub; rare and endangered in the Northeast. Shrikes are predatory songbirds. They impale large insects and small vertebrates on a thorn or barbed wire and then tear into them with their stout, hooked beaks. Any shrike seen in the North in winter is likely to be a **Northern Shrike**, a larger, paler species that wanders south irregularly from its subarctic nesting habitat.

MIMIC THRUSHES
AND SHRIKES

BROWN
THRASHER

GRAY
CATBIRD

NORTHERN
MOCKINGBIRD

LOGGERHEAD
SHRIKE

Mockingbird

Shrike

THRUSHES This widespread family of songbirds is characterized by a plump, rounded breast and alert, upright posture; includes the familiar American Robin and Eastern Bluebird (p. 116), plus the highly migratory "spotted" thrushes (see below). The "spotted" species, which nest in the shadowy undergrowth of woodlands and northern spruce forests, are most frequently observed as they pass through city parks and suburban gardens during migration. Their flutelike songs are among the most musical and ethereal sounds in nature, although they are seldom heard away from breeding grounds.

WOOD THRUSH *Hylocichla mustelina*. 8" (20 cm). Common thrush of eastern woodlands and the only species that nests in the Southeast. Distinguished from others by its rusty upperparts (brightest on the head) and bold spotting on the breast and belly. Also compare to the Brown Thrasher (p. 112) and the juvenile American Robin (p. 116). The Wood Thrush's song, commonly heard at twilight, alternates short, twinkling, flutelike phrases (3 to 5 notes) with a quick, higher-pitched trill or gurgle.

HERMIT THRUSH *Catharus guttatus*. 7" (18 cm). Brownish-olive back, shading to rust on the tail; finely spotted on the upper breast. Characteristically pumps its tail upward, then eases it back down. A common migrant in early spring and late fall and the only spotted thrush that winters in North America. Nests in northern coniferous forests and mixed woodlands at higher elevations. Widespread in winter in woodlands, parks, and thickets.

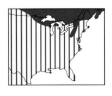

SWAINSON'S THRUSH *Catharus ustulatus*. 7" (18 cm). Uniform olive-brown above and finely spotted on the breast, with a bold buffy eye ring and buff tinge on the face. A common, widespread migrant. Nests in coniferous forests and at the higher elevations of the Appalachian Mountains. The very similar **Gray-cheeked Thrush** lacks the Swainson's eye ring and buff tones on the face and sides. Like Swainson's, it nests in spruce forests of the far North and on high peaks in the Northeast.

VEERY *Catharus fuscescens*. 7" (18 cm). Uniform rusty-brown above; breast is tinged pale buff with very faint spotting. Common migrant; nests in swampy woodlands and mixed forests. Its song is distinctive and easily recognized: a series of windy, flutelike notes spiraling down the scale. Call note is *veer*.

"SPOTTED" THRUSHES

WOOD THRUSH

HERMIT THRUSH

SWAINSON'S
THRUSH

GRAY-CHEEKED
THRUSH

VEERY

AMERICAN ROBIN *Turdus migratorius*. 10" (25 cm). Familiar red-breasted thrush of lawns and gardens. Also common in open woodlands, forest clearings, and pastures. Note the white corners on the tail, most noticeable in flight. Juvenile is spotted, but the rust tinge on the breast clearly suggests adult plumage. Robins migrate in large flocks. In spring they often arrive with the first hints of warm weather, swarming over recently thawed fields and yanking earthworms from the turf. Flocks may linger throughout the winter in the North, surviving in moist thickets and overgrown fields on a variety of wild fruits and berries. Song is a sequence of sweet, whistled phrases: *cheerio, cheerily, cheery, cheerio*, etc.

EASTERN BLUEBIRD *Sialia sialis*. 7" (18 cm). Glowing, blue-backed male is unmistakable. Blue tinges on female's wings and tail may be visible only in flight. Juvenile is speckled with white. Note distinctive shape and posture of bluebirds: pudgy and round-headed, they sit upright and slightly hunched. Locally common in farm country, orchards, and rural gardens, where they often perch on roadside fences and phone lines. Bluebirds prefer to nest in tree cavities but are often displaced by more aggressive, introduced species such as House Sparrows and European Starlings. Luckily, they readily accept birdhouses and today are most common where nest boxes have been provided. Small flocks may linger in the North during mild winters. The **Mountain Bluebird** is a Western species whose breeding range extends into the northern plains. The male is entirely azure-blue. (Female is grayer than Eastern female, with no rust on the breast.) In winter small flocks wander through the open southern prairies and central Texas; a rare vagrant farther East.

CEDAR WAXWING *Bombycilla cedrorum*. 7" (18 cm). Sleek and crested, with a distinctive black mask; has a yellow band on the tip of the tail. The name refers to small, waxy, red tips on the wing feathers of most adults. Juvenal plumage overlaid with blurry streaks. Locally common in semi-open country, Waxwings are highly gregarious and are almost never seen singly. Large nomadic flocks feed on berries in winter. In flight, Waxwings resemble Starlings; listen for their unique high, lisping calls as they pass overhead. The rare **Bohemian Waxwing**, a larger species with white in the wings and rusty undertail coverts, is an extremely rare visitor to the North in winter.

male

AMERICAN ROBIN

female

juvenile

male

EASTERN BLUEBIRD

male

MOUNTAIN BLUEBIRD

female

CEDAR WAXWING

THRUSHES AND WAXWINGS

GNATCATCHERS AND KINGLETS These tiny, energetic songbirds of woods and thickets are foliage gleaners, picking off small insects, larvae, and eggs from twigs and leaf surfaces with their thin, sharp bills.

BLUE-GRAY GNATCATCHER *Polioptila caerulea*. 4¾" (12 cm). Tiny and slender, with long tail; blue-gray above, paler below. Note the narrow white eye ring and white outer tail feathers. Females and nonbreeding males lack black crown markings. Common but inconspicuous summer residents of deciduous woodlands, especially in the South. They flit and flutter in the forest canopy, nervously cocking and twitching their tails and calling constantly. Call is a high, thin, whining *tzeee*.

RUBY-CROWNED KINGLET *Regulus calendula*. 4¼" (11 cm). Tiny, greenish-gray. Note broken white eye ring and dark patch just below wing bars. Male's red crown patch is usually hidden. An abundant and widespread migrant, it flits about constantly, frequently jerking its wings. Nests in boreal spruce forests, but in winter can be found in thickets and deciduous woods. Call a scratchy *je-dit*.

GOLDEN-CROWNED KINGLET *Regulus satrapa*. 4" (10 cm). Tiny and compact. Note bold white eyebrow and striped, colorful crown. A common fall migrant and winter resident, this species often associates with flocks of chickadees, nuthatches, and creepers. Nests in northern spruce forests and Appalachian highlands. Call a high, thin *tsee tsee tsee*.

VIREOS Small, mostly drab greenish or grayish songbirds, vireos are best told from kinglets, warblers, and small flycatchers by their heavier builds, thicker beaks, and more sluggish movements. Vireos are tireless songsters, but they tend to forage high in the forest canopy or deep within dense thickets and can be difficult to locate.

RED-EYED VIREO *Vireo olivaceous*. 6½" (16 cm). Best distinguished by its black-edged grayish crown and white eyebrow. The red eye is discernible only at close range. Very common but inconspicuous summer resident of suburban yards, parks, and deciduous forests. Its song of short, whistled phrases, repeated endlessly, is a familiar sound of summer. The **Warbling Vireo** is similar but grayer, marked only with a soft, pale eyebrow. A common summer resident throughout the East, it prefers large shade trees in parks and pastures and along roads, streams, and wooded edges. Song is a finchlike warble.

GNATCATCHER, KINGLETS, AND VIREOS

male

BLUE-GRAY
GNATCATCHER

female

RUBY-CROWNED
KINGLET

female

male

GOLDEN-CROWNED
KINGLET

male

RED-EYED
VIREO

WARBLING
VIREO

SOLITARY VIREO *Vireo solitarius*. 5½" (14 cm). A chunky, large-headed vireo with crisp white "spectacles" and wing bars. Also note the contrasting blue-gray head and the olive-green back, yellowish sides, and white throat and breast. A fairly common migrant in early spring and late fall; during summer it nests in coniferous groves (especially hemlock) within mixed northern forests. Its song is very similar to the Red-eyed Vireo's but sounds sweeter, with longer pauses between each phrase.

YELLOW-THROATED VIREO *Vireo flavifrons*. 5½" (14 cm). Similar to the Solitary Vireo in shape and habits but its throat, breast, and "spectacles" are bright yellow. Fairly common but inconspicuous summer resident of tall shade trees along roadsides and in deciduous woodlands and wooded edges. As with most vireos, the Yellow-throated Vireo is often heard long before it is found. Its song is like the Red-eyed's, but slower and with a distinctive nasal quality.

BELL'S VIREO *Vireo bellii*. 4¾" (12 cm). Small, active vireo of the Midwest and southern plains. Note the stout vireo bill, dark iris, faint eyebrow, and incomplete dingy white "spectacles." Plumage is somewhat variable. Most Bell's Vireos show one wing bar, although others may appear to have two. Uncommon and local summer resident of streamside willows and thickets. Forages low in dense brush. Song is a loud, harsh, and squeaky chatter.

WHITE-EYED VIREO *Vireo griseus*. 5" (13 cm). A compact vireo with diffuse yellow "spectacles" and diagnostic white iris. Also note the yellowish tinge on the sides and the white wing bars. Immatures have dark eyes. White-eyed Vireos forage among the lower branches of thickets and tangles, deftly keeping out of sight. Listen for their loud and rather strange song, *chick-a-perweeoo-chick*. Especially common in the South.

YELLOW-BREASTED CHAT *Icteria virens*. 7½" (19 cm). An odd and atypical wood-warbler, distinguished by its large size, long tail, and heavy beak. Note the plain dark olive upperparts, bold white "spectacles," and rich yellow throat and breast. Common in the South; quite local in the North. Chats inhabit dense thickets and overgrown fields and are difficult to observe, but their bizarre repertoire of harsh grunts, squeaks, and whistles is unmistakable.

SOLITARY VIREO

YELLOW-THROATED VIREO

BELL'S VIREO

WHITE-EYED VIREO

YELLOW-BREASTED CHAT

WOOD-WARBLERS These are small, energetic songbirds related to tanagers and finches. With the single exception of the Yellow-breasted Chat (p. 120), they have thin, sharp beaks adapted for eating small insects. In spring, most male wood-warblers are boldly patterned, brightly colored, and conspicuously vocal. During spring migration over 30 species may be observed as they pass through city parks and backyards. Most adult wood-warblers retain some recognizable semblance of this spring plumage during their quiet southward passage in late summer and fall. However, many autumn migrants are drab, obscurely patterned immature birds. While a few are confusing and difficult to identify, most immature warbler plumages subtly suggest their parents' characteristic pattern of markings and, with practice, can be identified in the field.

Although any of the species of wood-warblers that nest in eastern North America may be seen during migration, the species that are illustrated on this page are known almost exclusively as migrants. They nest in boreal or mixed forests north of our area and spend the winter months in Central and South America, but during brief periods of spring and fall (often just for a day or two), they may be quite common in woodlands, parks, and gardens. Included for comparison are immature plumages of many common breeding warblers (pp. 124 to 133) that may also be seen during fall migration.

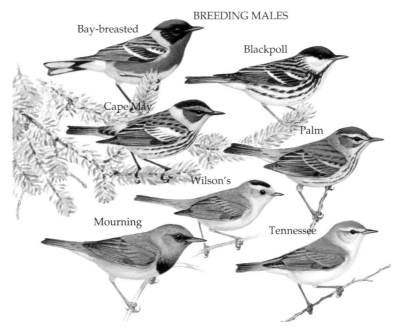

BREEDING MALES

Bay-breasted

Blackpoll

Cape May

Palm

Wilson's

Mourning

Tennessee

MIGRANT WARBLERS

FALL IMMATURES

Yellow-rumped

Blackburnian

Palm

Cape May

Black-throated Green

Blackpoll

Magnolia

Bay-breasted

Prairie

Pine

Nashville

Chestnut-sided

Canada

Tennessee

Mourning

Common Yellowthroat female

Orange-crowned

Yellow

Hooded

Wilson's

YELLOW WARBLER *Dendroica petechia*. 5" (13 cm). A bright yellow warbler with reddish breast streaks. Females and immatures are duller greenish yellow and unstreaked. Note the black "button" eye and the yellow spots on the inner webs of the tail feathers. Common and widespread in thickets, overgrown pastures, and marshy edges. Song a clear, ringing *sweet, sweet, sweet, sweeta-seeta-see*.

BLUE-WINGED WARBLER *Vermivora pinus*. 4¾" (12 cm). Small yellow warbler with bluish-gray wings, white wing bars, and a thin black eye line. Female similar but duller in color. Fairly common summer resident of overgrown pastures and second growth. Typical song is a descending, insectlike *bee-bzzzzz*. The strikingly patterned **Golden-winged Warbler** nests in similar habitats, but usually at higher elevations than the Blue-winged, and its range extends farther north. Where these species coexist, they interbreed, producing a variety of hybrids.

PRAIRIE WARBLER *Dendroica discolor*. 4¾" (12 cm). Male's facial pattern and streaks down sides of breast are distinctive; female and immature are duller (pp. 123, 132), but suggestion of male's facial pattern is usually evident. Common in dry, scrubby fields, second growth, and pine barrens. Resident population of coastal Florida inhabits mangroves. Unique song is an ascending series of buzzy, insectlike notes.

CHESTNUT-SIDED WARBLER *Dendroica pensylvanica*. 5" (13 cm). Breeding male is unmistakable. Female similar but duller, with some chestnut on sides. Immature is bright yellow-green above, with bold wing bars and a crisp white eye ring on its grayish face (p. 123). Common in young second growth, along roadsides, and in power-line cuts. Song is similar to Yellow Warbler's, typically: *swee, swee, swee, swee-SEE-yew!*

COMMON YELLOWTHROAT *Geothlypis trichas*. 5" (13 cm). Adult male, with his broad black mask, is distinctive. Drab brownish-olive female and immature are potentially confusing but always have yellow throats. Also note whitish belly and narrow, incomplete eye ring. Very common and widespread in marshy edges, wet meadows, and thickets, where it forages low among reeds and brambles. Song is a loud, clear series of triplets: *witchity, witchity, witchity*. Call is a harsh, abrupt *chit*.

male

Widespread in overgrown
fields, wet thickets, and
deciduous second growth

YELLOW WARBLER

female

PRAIRIE
WARBLER

BLUE-WINGED
WARBLER

male

male

CHESTNUT-SIDED
WARBLER

GOLDEN-WINGED
WARBLER

male

male

female

male

COMMON
YELLOWTHROAT

female

BREEDING WARBLERS I

NORTHERN PARULA *Parula americana.* 4½" (12 cm). Small bluish warbler with white wing bars and a yellow throat. Male has russet breast band. Immature is greenish above (p. 132). Most common in southern swamps where it nests in Spanish moss. In the North, Parulas nest in moist coniferous and mixed forests, usually in dangling clumps of lichen. Song is an ascending buzzy trill with a sneezy end: *zeezeezeezee-tzip!* The blue-backed **Cerulean Warbler**, uncommon and local in the canopy of deciduous bottomland forests, is told by its narrow black breast band. Female is blue-green above, whitish below, with a pale eyebrow and white wing bars.

YELLOW-THROATED WARBLER *Dendroica dominica.* 5¼" (14 cm). Both sexes boldly patterned gray, black, and white with a yellow throat. Common and widespread in the South along riverbanks, in swampy bottomlands, and in pine and oak woodlands. Forages along limbs of large trees. Song is clear and sweet: *see-u, seu, seu, seu, seuseu-swee.*

PINE WARBLER *Dendroica pinus.* 5¼" (14 cm). Unstreaked olive above, variably yellow on throat and breast, with white wing bars and whitish belly and undertail coverts. Female similar but duller. Aptly named resident of open pinewoods and barrens; common in the South but quite local in the North. Winters in most of the Southeast, and may visit feeders (see also p. 132). Song, a slow, modulating trill, suggests Chipping Sparrow's.

PROTHONOTARY WARBLER *Protonotaria citrea.* 5½" (14 cm). Bright golden-yellow warbler of swamps and flooded bottomlands. Note the blue-gray wings and tail and white tail spots. Female similar but duller. Common summer resident in appropriate habitat throughout the South. Nests in rotted stumps or tree cavities. Song is a clear, monotonic *sweet, sweet, sweet, sweet.*

HOODED WARBLER *Wilsonia citrina.* 5½" (14 cm). Adult male unmistakable. Female told by yellow face set off by olive-green cowl. Note also the white tail spots that flash conspicuously when it flicks its tail. Common in the dense, leafy undergrowth of moist woodlands, ravines, and swampy bottomlands. Its song is sweet and spirited, often transcribed as *weeta, weeta, wee-TEE-o.* Also common in moist southern forests is the furtive **Kentucky Warbler**. Its loud song resonates from the shadowy undergrowth: *churwee, churwee, churwee.*

BREEDING WARBLERS II

Mostly in Southern swamps, bottomlands, and pinewoods

NORTHERN PARULA

male

female

CERULEAN WARBLER

male

PINE WARBLER

male

ELLOW-THROATED WARBLER

sexes alike

female

HOODED WARBLER

male

female

PROTHONOTARY WARBLER

female

male

male

KENTUCKY WARBLER

AMERICAN REDSTART *Setophaga ruticilla.* 5¼" (1 cm). Flashy black and orange adult males are unmistakable. Females and immatures have pale yellow patches on the tails, wings, and sides (tinged orange on young males). Common and widespread. Redstarts flutter through the forest, flicking their wings, splaying their tails, and darting out like a flycatcher to snatch insects. Song is high and thin: *see, see, see, see, sew!*

BLACK-AND-WHITE WARBLER *Mniotilta varia.* 5¼ (13 cm). Boldly streaked black and white; best identified by tree-clinging behavior. Creeps on tree trunks and along inner branches like a nuthatch. Common and widespread in most wooded habitats. Song is high-pitched, monotonic series of couplets: *see-wee, see-wee, see-wee,* etc.

BLACK-THROATED BLUE WARBLER *Dendroica caerulescens.* 5¼" (13 cm). Male is unmistakable. Female drab brownish-olive, darkest on the cheek, with small white wing spot and narrow whitish eyebrow. Fairly common and widespread in mixed woodlands. Song a thick, wheezy *shur, shur, shur, shreeee.*

WORM-EATING WARBLER *Helmitheros vermivorus.* 5½" (14 cm). Both sexes pale olive above, with black-striped crowns and buff underparts. Fairly common but inconspicuous summer resident of wooded hillsides and ravines. Song is a thin, insectlike trill.

OVENBIRD *Seiurus aurocapillus.* 6" (15 cm). Plump thrushlike warbler; olive above, streaked below, with a conspicuous white eye ring and black-bordered orange crown stripe. Widespread and common, Ovenbirds forage on the forest floor with a deliberate, bobbing gait and announce their presence with a ringing crescendo: *teacher, Teacher, TEACHER, **TEACHER**!*

LOUISIANA WATERTHRUSH *Seiurus motacilla.* 6" (15 cm). This thrushlike warbler of wooded streams has dark brown upperparts and a bold white eyebrow. Widespread and locally common in appropriate habitat. The very similar **Northern Waterthrush** nests farther north in bogs and wooded swamps. It is distinguished from the Louisiana by its shorter, tapering yellowish eyebrow, pale yellowish underparts, and finely spotted throat. During spring migration both species are commonly observed along watercourses in city parks, bobbing and teetering like Spotted Sandpipers.

BREEDING WARBLERS III

Widespread in deciduous woodlands

male

AMERICAN REDSTART

female

male

BLACK-AND-WHITE WARBLER

female

female

BLACK-THROATED BLUE WARBLER

male

WORM-EATING WARBLER

OVENBIRD

NORTHERN WATERTHRUSH

LOUISIANA WATERTHRUSH

Approximate range map for Warblers on this page.

BLACKBURNIAN WARBLER *Dendroica fusca*. 5" (13 cm). Adult male black and white with fiery-orange throat and head stripes. Female and immature duller but similar in pattern; throat and head stripes yellowish. Common but can be easily overlooked. Look for Blackburnians in treetops and listen for the distinctive trailing end of their song, a thin, ascending *tzeeeee?* that breezes up out of the audible range.

BLACK-THROATED GREEN WARBLER *Dendroica virens*. 5" (13 cm). Bright green back, yellow face, and black throat distinguish breeding male. Black throat less extensive on female; often no black at all on immature. Common and widespread, but tends to stay in the forest canopy and is more often heard than seen. Song is a wheezy *zee zee zee zoo shree* or *tzoo tzee tzootzoo tzit*. Easier to see during migration, when it also forages lower in thickets and woodland edges. A separate population nests in swamps of the coastal Southeast.

MAGNOLIA WARBLER *Dendroica magnolia*. 5" (13 cm). Adult male has broadly streaked yellow underparts, broken white tail band, and yellow rump. Female similar in pattern but duller. Immature (p. 123) faintly streaked, with indistinct grayish breast band. Common migrant; forages in leafy foliage of gardens, woodlands, and thickets. Nests in young conifers in clearings and cut-over areas. Song is loud, clear *sweeta, sweeta, sweet-eo*. The boldly patterned **Yellow-rumped Warbler** also flashes a yellow rump and white in the tail, but its underparts are white, densely streaked with black, and it has yellow patches on the sides of its breast. A common and widespread summer resident of mixed and coniferous forests (see map and additional text on p. 132).

CANADA WARBLER *Wilsonia canadensis*. 5½" (14 cm). Unique pattern: unmarked blue-gray above, bright yellow below, with bold "spectacles" and a "necklace" of short black streaks. Females and young similar but duller, with fainter breast streaks. Fairly common in the lush undergrowth of wet clearings and streamside thickets.

NASHVILLE WARBLER *Vermivora ruficapilla* . 4¾" (12 cm). Crisp, circular white eye ring and grayish helmet contrast with greenish back, yellow throat, and yellow underparts. Fairly common in the undergrowth of bogs, thickets, and clearings. Song like Yellow Warbler's but in two distinct parts: *tsebit, tsebit, tsebit*, followed by a short trill.

130

BREEDING WARBLERS IV

Widespread in Northern
coniferous forests and
Appalachian highlands

male

BLACKBURNIAN
WARBLER

female

male

BLACK-
THROATED
GREEN WARBLER

female

MAGNOLIA
WARBLER

male

YELLOW-RUMPED
WARBLER

male

male

CANADA
WARBLER

female

NASHVILLE
WARBLER

male

YELLOW-RUMPED WARBLER *Dendroica coronata*
5½" (14 cm). The only warbler commonly seen in winter in the North. Locally abundant; loose flocks forage in bayberry scrub and marshy hollows among coastal dunes and on barrier islands. Occasionally seen at bird feeders. Note the yellow rump (conspicuous in flight) and yellowish smudges on the sides of the breast. Call note a dry *check*. Common and widespread migrant in early spring and late fall. (See also p. 130.) Eastern subspecies was formerly known as the Myrtle Warbler.

NORTHERN PARULA *Parula americana*. 4½" (12 cm) May be seen in extreme southern Florida in winter (See also p. 126.)

PALM WARBLER *Dendroica palmarum*. 5¼" (13 cm). Drab brownish-olive warbler with a pale eyebrow and yellow undertail coverts. Usually forages near the ground; constantly pumps its tail. Widespread late-fall migrant and fairly common winter resident of weedy fields, marshy edges, coastal dunes, and scrub. Compare with immature Yellow-rumped. Breeding plumage shown on p. 122.

PINE WARBLER *Dendroica pinus*. 5¼" (14 cm). A large drab greenish warbler, with white wing bars and undertail coverts and a large beak. Year-round resident in pinewoods. (See also p. 126.)

PRAIRIE WARBLER *Dendroica discolor*. 4¾" (12 cm). Yellow-breasted in all plumages, with pattern of dark streaks on face and sides. Fairly common winter resident in Florida. (See also p. 124.)

ORANGE-CROWNED WARBLER *Vermivora celata*. 5" (13 cm). Drab grayish-olive with pale yellow undertail coverts and variable blurry streaks on breast. Note the thin, broken eye ring and obscure dark line through the eye. The dull orange crown patch is rarely seen. Immatures are grayer with just a hint of yellow under the tail (p. 123). Fairly common winter resident of thickets and brushy woodland edges, especially along the Gulf Coast and in Florida; rare migrant in the Northeast. Call note a sharp, sparrowlike *tsip*.

COMMON YELLOWTHROAT *Geothlypis trichas*. 5" (13 cm). Common year-round resident of wet tangles and marshy habitats throughout the South. (See also p. 124.)

WINTERING WARBLERS

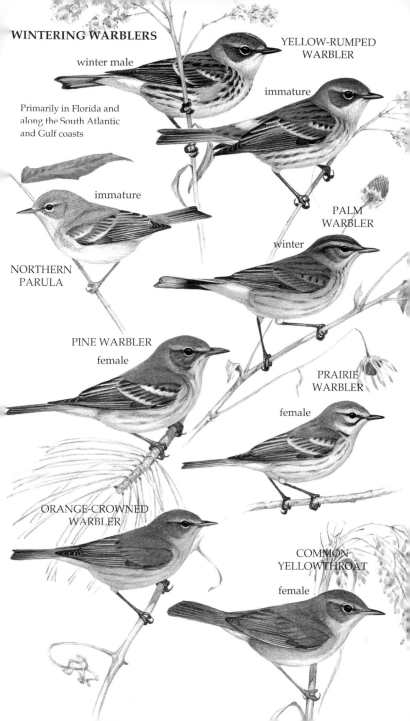

YELLOW-RUMPED WARBLER

winter male

immature

Primarily in Florida and along the South Atlantic and Gulf coasts

immature

NORTHERN PARULA

PALM WARBLER

winter

PINE WARBLER

female

PRAIRIE WARBLER

female

ORANGE-CROWNED WARBLER

COMMON YELLOWTHROAT

female

BLACKBIRDS (Icterids) A diverse New World group related to tanagers, grosbeaks, and warblers, blackbirds include the brightly colored orioles (p. 138), glossy black grackles, cowbirds (p. 136), and cryptically patterned meadowlarks. The most consistent family trait is the shape of the beak—tapered, conical, and sharply pointed.

BOBOLINK *Dolichonyx oryzivorus*. 7" (18 cm). Gregarious summer resident of hayfields, meadows, and prairies. Uniquely patterned breeding males are black below, buff and white above. Their bubbly song, often uttered during a frenzied courtship flight, sounds like a jumble of touch-tone phone signals. Females, immatures, and nonbreeding males resemble large sparrows; note the crown stripes, rich buff color, and pointed tail feathers. In fall, migrating Bobolinks may forage on marshes and in weedy thickets.

EASTERN MEADOWLARK *Sturnella magna*. 9¾" (25 cm). Plump, short-tailed blackbird with a long, tapered beak and flat-headed profile. Frontal view reveals bright yellow breast with black V. Meadowlarks fly with shallow wingbeats; note their white outer tail feathers. Common and widespread in open country; most often seen perched on roadside wires and fence posts. Song a clear, sweet, deliberate whistle: *tsee-you tsee-year*. The nearly identical **Western Meadowlark,** common in grassland and agricultural areas eastward to the Mississippi, is best distinguished by its song: a liquid series of rich, flutelike notes, lower in pitch and more complex than the Eastern's song.

RED-WINGED BLACKBIRD *Agelaius phoeniceus*. 8¾" (22 cm). Jet-black with scarlet epaulets, males are unmistakable. Females, dark brownish and densely streaked, are best distinguished by their size and sharp, tapered beaks. Young males resemble females, but are darker, with some reddish-orange on their shoulders. Familiar breeding resident of marshes, wet thickets, ponds, and prairie potholes. Song is a shrill, fluid *konk-la-reee*. In fall and winter, Red-wings often gather in noisy flocks with Starlings and other blackbirds to forage in fields and on marshes.

YELLOW-HEADED BLACKBIRD *Xanthocephalus xanthocephalus*. 9¾" (25 cm). A striking blackbird of prairie marshes and cattails. Female is much smaller than male and best identified by her unstreaked pale throat and yellowish breast. Nests in large, noisy colonies, and often flocks with other blackbirds in nonbreeding season. Rare in the East.

BLACKBIRDS OF MEADOW AND MARSH

BOBOLINK

male

female

EASTERN
MEADOWLARK

male

RED-WINGED
BLACKBIRD

male

YELLOW-HEADED
BLACKBIRD

immature male

female

female

EUROPEAN STARLING *Sturnus vulgaris.* 8½" (22 cm). Familiar, rambunctious resident of cities, suburban yards, farms, and roadsides. Breeding adults have iridescent gloss and yellow beaks; winter plumage speckled with white; beak dusky. Juveniles are brownish. Note the distinctive flight silhouette: compact and short-tailed, with short, triangular wings. Not true Icterids, Starlings were introduced from Europe in 1890; they are now abundant throughout North America.

BROWN-HEADED COWBIRD *Molothrus ater.* 7½" (19 cm). Smaller than other blackbirds. Male is shiny blue-black with a brown head. Female is brownish-gray with a conical, finchlike beak. Common and widespread in open country, especially around farms. Cowbirds are *brood parasites*; the female lays eggs in other birds' nests, and the young Cowbirds are raised by the foster parents.

BREWER'S BLACKBIRD *Euphagus cyanocephalus.* 9¼" (24 cm). Male glossy black with a pale iris; smaller and shorter-tailed than Common Grackle. Female dark brownish-gray with a dark iris; beak thinner and more tapered than Cowbird's. Common summer resident of the northern Great Plains near farms, towns, and roadsides. Uncommon in the Southeast in winter.

RUSTY BLACKBIRD *Euphagus carolinus.* 9¼" (24 cm). Slender blackbird of northern bogs and wooded swamps. Breeding male closely resembles Brewer's, but seldom occurs in same habitat during summer; breeding female slate-gray with a pale iris. Most easily identified in its unique "rusty" fall plumage.

COMMON GRACKLE *Quiscalus quiscula.* 11" (28 cm) to 13½" (35 cm). Sleek, iridescent blackbird with a long, wedge-shaped tail and pale iris; larger and longer-tailed than Brewer's and Rusty Blackbirds. Common in city parks, suburban yards, woodlands, and farm fields. Gregarious, except when nesting; often flocks with other kinds of blackbirds.

BOAT-TAILED GRACKLE *Quiscalus major.* Male 16½" (42 cm), female 13" (33 cm). Large grackle of coastal marshes from eastern Texas to New York. Beak and tail are proportionately longer than Common Grackle's. Female smaller than male and brownish. In Texas and the southern plains, the nearly identical but larger **Great-tailed Grackle** has been expanding its range. Most Boat-tailed along the Atlantic coast also show a pale iris.

EUROPEAN STARLING

juvenile

BROWN-HEADED COWBIRD

male

female

winter

summer

RUSTY BLACKBIRD

fall male

BREWER'S BLACKBIRD

male

"Purple" subspecies

female

COMMON GRACKLE

"Bronzed" subspecies

male

BOAT-TAILED GRACKLE

dark-eyed Gulf Coast form

female

STARLING AND "BLACK" BLACKBIRDS

NORTHERN ORIOLE *Icterus galbula*. 7¾" (20 cm). Adult males unmistakable. Females and immatures dull yellow-orange below, brownish-olive above, with pale wing bars and slender, pointed beaks. Some females have blackish mottling on the head that may suggest the male's hooded pattern. Eastern subspecies was formerly known as the "Baltimore" Oriole. The "Bullock's" Oriole of the West ranges east into the Great Plains, where the two forms interbreed. Common in woodlands, parks, and suburbs. Oriole nests, which dangle from the outer twigs of shade trees, are exquisitely woven pouches of plant fibers and animal hair. Song a series of sweet, whistled notes.

ORCHARD ORIOLE *Icterus spurius*. 7" (18 cm). Male boldly patterned black and chestnut. Female is greenish-yellow; smaller than female Northern Oriole, with no hint of orange in the plumage. Also more delicately proportioned than tanager, with straighter, finely tapered beak. Young male is similar with black mask and throat. Locally fairly common in orchards and pastures and along roadsides; most common in the South.

TANAGERS These are, generally, brilliantly colored songbirds of neotropical forests; two species nest in eastern North America. Their beaks are thick and bluntly pointed—shaped somewhere between an oriole's pointed beak and the short, conical bill of a bunting.

SCARLET TANAGER *Piranga olivacea*. 7" (18 cm). Breeding male is scarlet red with velvet-black wings and tail. Female dull olive-yellow, distinguished from sleeker female orioles and much smaller wood-warblers and vireos by her thick beak, unmarked dark wings, and sluggish behavior. Nonbreeding male resembles female but retains black wings and may be splotched with red while molting. Common but surprisingly inconspicuous summer resident of deciduous forests and wooded suburbs; usually forages high in the forest canopy. Distinctive call is a burry *chip-churr;* song is like Robin's but hoarser.

SUMMER TANAGER *Piranga rubra*. 7½" (19 cm). Male entirely red, with stout pale beak. Female golden yellow, tinged olive on the back and wings (some may also be suffused with orange-red); told from female Scarlet Tanager by her heavier bill and deeper ochre hues. Fairly common breeding resident of southern woodlands; rare but regular spring vagrant in the North. Call is a loud, sharp *pik-i-tuck* or *pi-tuck;* song is Robin-like.

oriole at nest

male

NORTHERN ORIOLE

"Baltimore" subspecies

female

"Bullock's" subspecies

male

male

female

ORCHARD ORIOLE

immature male

nonbreeding male

breeding male

female

SCARLET TANAGER

male

female

SUMMER TANAGER

ORIOLES AND TANAGERS

ROSE-BREASTED GROSBEAK *Pheucticus ludovicianus.* 8" (20 cm). Breeding males unmistakable; in flight, their white rumps and wing patches and pink wing linings are flashy and conspicuous. Females and nonbreeding males suggest oversized sparrows or female Purple Finches, with huge beaks and yellow wing linings. Common in deciduous woodlands, parks, and rural gardens. Song is a rich, Robin-like warble; call note is a squeaky, metallic *eek*. This species' Western counterpart, the **Black-headed Grosbeak**, breeds east into the northern and central plains. Breeding males are distinctive; females are nearly identical to Rose-breasted but buffier and less streaked below.

INDIGO BUNTING *Passerina cyanea.* 5½" (14 cm). Small; breeding males deep, shining blue (but often appear blackish in poor light). Females and nonbreeding males are plain, warm brown, often with a hint of blue in the wings and tails. Common breeding resident of overgrown fields, clearings, and woodland edges. Males sing from a conspicuous perch. This species' Western counterpart, the **Lazuli Bunting**, breeds in similar habitats of the western Great Plains. Male Lazulis are unmistakable; females very similar to female Indigos, with pale wing bars.

PAINTED BUNTING *Passerina ciris.* 5¼" (13 cm). Small, multicolored finch of southern thickets, gardens, and roadsides. Females are apple-green above, our only small greenish songbird with a conical bill. Local along the Atlantic coast; most common in Gulf Coast states. Regular winter visitor at feeders in southern Florida.

BLUE GROSBEAK *Guiraca caerulea.* 7" (18 cm). Male deep blue with rusty wing bars; female plain, warm brown with cinnamon wing bars. Fairly common in southern brush, farmlands, wet thickets, and woodland edges. Often seen on roadside wires and fences. Told from Brown-headed Cowbird (p. 136) or smaller Buntings by the broad wing bars and heavy beak.

NORTHERN CARDINAL *Cardinalis cardinalis.* 8½" (22 cm). Familiar crested red finch of suburban gardens, parks, brushy clearings, and thickets. Tawny-brown female identified by orange-red beak and red tinges on the wings, tail, and crest (juveniles in late summer have a dark beak). Call note a sharp, metallic *teep;* song is a series of clear, loud, slurred whistles: *tew, tew, tew* or *whoit, whoit, whoit.*

GROSBEAKS AND BUNTINGS

ROSE-BREASTED GROSBEAK

breeding male

female

Rose-breasted

male

BLACK-HEADED GROSBEAK

LAZULI BUNTING

male

INDIGO BUNTING

breeding male

PAINTED BUNTING

female

female

BLUE GROSBEAK

male

male

female

female

NORTHERN CARDINAL

male

RUFOUS-SIDED TOWHEE *Pipilo erythrophthalmus*. 8" (21 cm). Large, boldly patterned "sparrow" of overgrown fields, thickets, open woodlands, and garden edges. Common but hard to spot as it forages under bushes and tangles, loudly rustling among fallen leaves. Call is an inquisitive *cha-wee?* Song is loud and metallic, often transcribed as *drink your tea-eeee*. Juvenile is streaked and sparrowlike, but its wing and tail are like the adult's.

FIELD SPARROW *Spizella pusilla*. 5½" (14 cm). Slender clean-breasted sparrow with a rusty cap, small pink bill, grayish face, and narrow white eye ring. Common but inconspicuous in overgrown pastures and brushy clearings. Its presence is often revealed only by its tirelessly repeated song, a series of sweet whistled notes accelerating into a loose trill, rising slightly in pitch. *seeyew, seeyew, sew sew sew su susususyew?*

CHIPPING SPARROW *Spizella passerina*. 5¼" (14 cm). In breeding plumage a trim, clean-breasted sparrow with a rusty cap, black bill, and combination black eye line and white eyebrow. Familiar summer resident of rural gardens, parks, and semi-open country. Song is loud monotone trill of chips. In fall and winter, adult and immature Chipping Sparrows have a finely streaked brownish crown and resemble the **Clay-colored Sparrow**, a prairie species that nests in brushy clearings of the northern plains. Clay-colored is best identified by its brown face patch, framed by the pale lores, bright white eyebrow, and malar stripe.

AMERICAN TREE SPARROW *Spizella arborea*. 6¼" (16 cm). Winter counterpart of the Chipping Sparrow throughout most of the North. Fairly large and long-tailed, with a rusty cap and eye line, yellow lower mandible, and gray breast punctuated by a dark central spot. Common in weedy fields and thickets and may visit backyard feeders in rural areas. Gregarious; often flocks with Juncos. Call is a cheerful, liquid *tsewlee*.

DARK-EYED JUNCO *Junco hyemalis*. 6¼" (16 cm). Slate-gray with white outer tail feathers that flash conspicuously in flight and a white belly. Abundant winter resident of woods, thickets, roadsides, parks, and yards. Nests in undergrowth of northern mixed coniferous forests. Call a series of sharp, staccato *chips*. Widespread and variable; flocks wintering on the Great Plains may include birds of the distinctive Western subspecies, such as the black-hooded "Oregon" Junco.

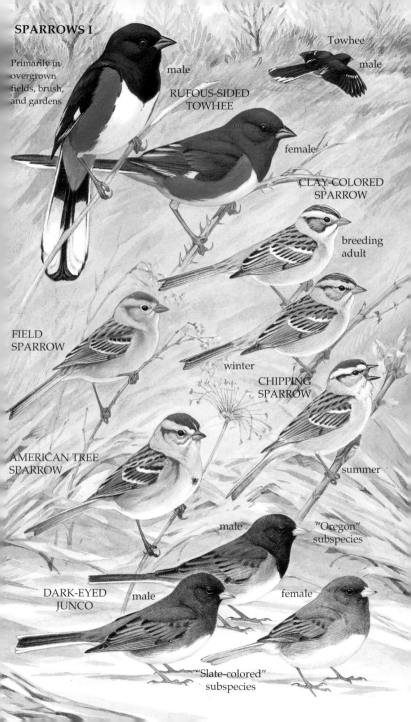

SPARROWS I

Primarily in overgrown fields, brush, and gardens

male

Towhee

male

RUFOUS-SIDED TOWHEE

female

CLAY-COLORED SPARROW

breeding adult

FIELD SPARROW

winter

CHIPPING SPARROW

AMERICAN TREE SPARROW

summer

male

"Oregon" subspecies

DARK-EYED JUNCO

male

female

"Slate-colored" subspecies

WHITE-CROWNED SPARROW *Zonotrichia leu-cophrysa*. 7" (18 cm). Identified by crisp black and white crown stripes, pink bill, clean gray underparts, and perky, upright posture (obvious when seen in mixed flocks with White-throated Sparrows). Immature has buff and brown crown stripes. Fairly common migrant and winter resident of brushy thickets, woodland edges, parks, and gardens. Uncommon in the Northeast.

WHITE-THROATED SPARROW *Zonotrichia albicollis*. 6¾" (17 cm). Occurs in two morphs: one crowned with black and white stripes, the other with buff and brown stripes. Both have unstreaked grayish breasts, sharply delineated white throats, and bright yellow lores. Immature resembles tan morph, but dingier with streaks on the breast. Widespread and familiar migrant and winter resident of woodlands, thickets, brushy fields, and backyards; common at feeders. Nests in mixed coniferous forests of the North. Song easily recognized: 3 to 5 musical whistles, often transcribed as *ola sam peabody peabody*. Call note is *tseet*. Wintering flocks in the central and southern plains may include the related **Harris' Sparrow**. Note its large size, pink bill, and blackish head pattern.

SWAMP SPARROW *Melospiza georgiana*. 5½" (14 cm). A dark, rusty sparrow; identified by combination of rusty crown (brown in winter), whitish throat, gray breast, and cinnamon flanks. Common in northern bogs, swamps, and cattails, but furtive and inconspicuous; in winter also found in wet thickets and weedy tangles.

SONG SPARROW *Melospiza melodia*. 6¼" (16 cm). Widespread and variable; generally, heavily streaked grayish-brown to rust, with a long, rounded tail, dark convergence of streaks in the center of its breast, and dark mustache marks. Our most familiar sparrow; common, especially near water, in thickets, brushy fields, backyards, and along roadsides. Call note an unemphatic *chimp*. Song a sweet, variable trill following 2 or 3 introductory notes; easily recognized once learned. Compare with the streaked, grassland species on p. 146.

FOX SPARROW *Passerella iliaca*. 7" (18 cm). Large, heavily streaked, rust-colored sparrow. Note central breast spot, bright rusty tail, and contrasting gray sides of the face. Uncommon migrant and winter resident in dense thickets and brush; may also visit feeders.

SPARROWS II

Widespread in gardens, wet thickets, and woodland edges

WHITE-CROWNED SPARROW

immature

adult

HARRIS' SPARROW

winter adult

white-striped morph

immature

WHITE-THROATED SPARROW

adult

winter

SWAMP SPARROW

SONG SPARROW

summer

FOX SPARROW

Eastern subspecies

GRASSHOPPER SPARROW *Ammodramus savan narum.* 5" (13 cm). Small, short-tailed sparrow of dry weedy pastures, hayfields, and grasslands. Keeps low in the grass, perching in the open only to sing its buzzy insectlike trill. Appears flat-headed with an oversized bill. Also note its unstreaked buffy breast. Uncommon and declining in the East; locally common on the Great Plains.

SAVANNAH SPARROW *Passerculus sandwichensis.* 5½" (14 cm). Common and widespread; a streaked sparrow of hayfields, prairies, grassy coastal dunes, and salt marshes; told by its short tail, striped crown, yellowish lores, and neatly streaked underparts. On some, the streaks may merge into a small central spot, suggesting the Song Sparrow (p. 144), which has a longer tail and a grayish eyebrow. Along the edges of salt marshes and prairie wetlands, the Savannah's dry, grassy habitat abuts the short marsh grass preferred by the furtive **Sharp-tailed Sparrow**. The Sharp-tailed has a dark crown and a distinctive gray cheek patch broadly bordered with bright orange-buff.

VESPER SPARROW *Pooecetes gramineus.* 6" (16 cm). Finely streaked, grayish-brown sparrow of farm fields, roadsides, and dry prairies. Most easily identified when it flies, flashing its conspicuous white outer feathers. Up close, look for the thin white eye ring and obscure rusty patch at the bend of the wing. Fairly common in appropriate habitat but declining in East. Comparable open-country birds are illustrated on p. 149.

LARK SPARROW *Chondestes grammacus.* 6¼" (16 cm). Large open-country sparrow with an unmistakable harlequin face, unstreaked breast with a dark central spot, and flashy white corners on its rounded tail. Locally common west of the Mississippi along roadsides and on agricultural fields, rangeland, and prairies.

DICKCISSEL *Spiza americana.* 6¼" (16 cm). Distinctive sparrowlike finch of the Great Plains. Male easily identified by black bib on his yellow breast. Female suggests female House Sparrow (p. 152), but note rusty wing coverts, faint malar streak, and yellow tinges on the face and breast. Gregarious; locally abundant in grainfields, hayfields, and weedy patches. Breeding males may sing from roadside fences, posts, or tall weed stalks. Song is a stuttering, buzzy rendering of its name: *tsick tsick tsick-zizizil.*

SPARROWS III

Primarily of fields, marshes, and prairies

GRASSHOPPER
SPARROW

SHARP-TAILED
SPARROW

SAVANNAH
SPARROW

Vesper

Lark

Song Sparrow
p. 144

VESPER
SPARROW

LARK
SPARROW

DICKCISSEL

male

female

AMERICAN PIPIT *Anthus rubescens*. 6½" (17 cm). Fairly common but local migrant and winter resident on plowed fields, beaches, and other open country. Terrestrial; usually seen in small flocks. Sparrowlike, but note slender build and thin bill. Tail has white edges and is bobbed and pumped as the bird walks. Call notes a thin *jeet* or *tzezeet*.

HORNED LARK *Eremophila alpestris*. 7½" (19 cm). Common and widespread in open country, especially on the Great Plains. Note the black tail with white edges, dark slash across the breast, and pied face pattern. Flocks with Snow Buntings and Lapland Longspurs in winter. Larks walk rather than hop. Call is a high, sibilant *zeewee* or *zeetiti*.

SNOW BUNTING *Plectrophenax nivalis*. 6½" (17 cm). Widespread winter resident of beaches, prairies, plowed fields, and other open country. Identified by its flashy white and black wings; flocks in flight seem to sparkle as they wheel and turn in unison. The rusty feather edgings of winter plumage gradually wear off, exposing a stark black and white breeding plumage (seldom seen south of the Arctic). Calls are a soft, whistled *tewloo* and a soft rattle. Search among flocks of Snow Buntings and Horned Larks for the smaller, darker **Lapland Longspur**. In winter, longspurs are sparrowlike and often overlooked. Lapland has dark marks bordering the ear patch, rusty wing coverts, and, on males, a dark smudge on the breast and rusty nape. Common in the Central Plains; scarce elsewhere.

CHESTNUT-COLLARED LONGSPUR *Calcarius ornatus*. 6" (15 cm). This is the only breeding longspur likely to be seen by the beginner. Males, which sing from rocks, fences, or tall grass stalks, are unmistakable. Females are drab and sparrowlike but are usually seen in flocks with males. In all plumages, the tail is white, marked with a distinctive dark triangle. Locally common in grassy prairies and rangeland of the northern Great Plains.

LARK BUNTING *Calamospiza melanocorys*. 6¾" (18 cm). Flashy, gregarious finch of short-grass prairies, sagebrush, and grasslands. Breeding male black with white wing patches (compare to Bobolink, p. 134). Female and immature are streaked brownish with a suggestion of male's wing patch and a stout grayish bill; nonbreeding male is similar but grayer, with a black chin.

PIPITS, LARKS, AND MISCELLANEOUS OPEN-COUNTRY FINCHES

Snow Buntings

Horned Lark

winter

breeding

northern subspecies

female

males

AMERICAN PIPIT

HORNED LARK

LAPLAND LONGSPUR

winter male

prairie subspecies

CHESTNUT-COLLARED LONGSPUR

winter male

SNOW BUNTING

breeding male

female

winter female

breeding male

LARK BUNTING

female

AMERICAN GOLDFINCH *Carduelis tristis*. 5" (13 cm). Familiar small yellow finch with a black forehead and black and white wings and tail. Female is dull greenish-yellow with a white rump and a pink conical beak, which helps to distinguish her from comparably sized warblers. Widespread in weedy fields, parks, and gardens. In winter both sexes resemble female but are tinged brown or grayish, with dusky beaks. Usually seen in small flocks, often with Siskins. Common at feeders, especially those offering thistle seed. Like that of most finches, its flight is undulating, with a dip between each wingbeat. Call is a sweet, twittering *po-tato-chips*.

PINE SISKIN *Carduelis pinus*. 5" (13 cm). Small, streaked winter finch typically seen in noisy, nomadic flocks. Suggests a Goldfinch in shape and size, but note the narrower, sharply pointed bill and yellow flashes in the wings and tail. Locally common in mixed and coniferous woodlands, along brushy roadsides, and at feeders. Distinctive call is a shrill, wheezy *zhreeee*. Breeds in mixed or coniferous northern forests; migratory movements are erratic and unpredictable.

COMMON REDPOLL *Carduelis flammea*. 5¼" (13 cm). Shaped like a Goldfinch and streaked like a Siskin, with a red cap, black chin, and rosy breast. This small Arctic finch is an erratic winter visitor across the northern states. Forages in wooded edges and weedy fields, and also visits feeders, often with Goldfinches.

PURPLE FINCH *Carpodacus purpureus*. 6" (14 cm). Stocky, bull-headed finch with a slightly peaked crown, thick, conical beak, and short, deeply notched tail. Male's plumage is suffused with rich raspberry red, brightest on the head. Female is heavily streaked with a broad dark malar streak and a pale eyebrow that starts behind the eye. Fairly common migrant and winter visitor in woodlands and rural gardens. Call is a soft, staccato *pic*.

HOUSE FINCH *Carpodacus mexicanus*. 5½" (14 cm). Native to the Southwest; introduced in the East in the 1940s and now abundant in city parks, in suburbs, on farmland, and at feeders. Male streaked brownish with red patches on head, breast, and rump. Densely streaked female lacks Purple Finch's bold head pattern. Shape is slender and longer-tailed than Purple's; tail is narrow and square-tipped. Call note a squeaky *cheeup*.

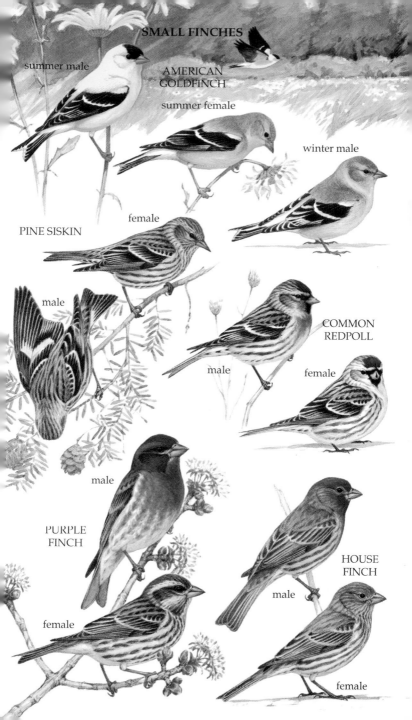

SMALL FINCHES

summer male

AMERICAN
GOLDFINCH

summer female

winter male

PINE SISKIN

female

male

COMMON
REDPOLL

male

female

PURPLE
FINCH

male

HOUSE
FINCH

male

female

female

WINTER FINCHES Pine and Evening Grosbeaks, Crossbills, Siskins, and Redpolls are called "winter" finches. In some years, these species wander southward from their northern breeding grounds. Foraging in nomadic flocks, they feed on seeds and berries in coniferous forests and mixed woodlands. Some species also visit backyard feeders.

RED CROSSBILL *Loxia curvirostra*. 6" (16 cm). Male dull brick-red with blackish wings and a short, notched dark tail. Female dull olive with dark wings and tail. Note its unique beak with crossed tips, adapted to extract conifer seeds from cones. Call a repeated *kip* or *jip*. The **White-winged Crossbill**, similar in behavior and shape, has bold white wing bars. Males are rosy-pink. Both species are uncommon and erratic in occurrence.

PINE GROSBEAK *Pinicola enucleator*. 9" (23 cm). Large, stocky finch with a short stubby bill. Rosy-red male is unmistakable; female is gray with an olive-ochre head and rump. Note the long, notched tail and blackish wings with narrow white edgings and wing bars. Infrequent irruptions bring flocks of these northern finches south to feed in mixed woodlands and parks. Call is a soft, whistled *tew, tew, tew*.

EVENING GROSBEAK *Coccothraustes vespertinus*. 8" (20 cm). Large, raucous winter finch. Male unmistakable; female similar but silvery gray with touches of yellow. Goldfinch has similar plumage but is much smaller. Locally common in mixed woodlands and clearings and at feeders, where they voraciously consume sunflower seeds. Flocks are nomadic and unpredictable but so noisy that they are impossible to miss. Call is a loud, grating *pleeer*, suggestive of House Sparrow's.

HOUSE SPARROW *Passer domesticus*. 6¼" (16 cm). Not a true finch but an Old World Sparrow (Weaver), introduced from Europe last century; now abundant throughout North America. This is the familiar sparrow of city streets, suburbs, and farmyards. Male's black bib, gray crown, and chestnut nape are distinctive. Drab female is unstreaked grayish below and streaked black and buff on the back, with a pale ochre eyebrow starting behind her eye. Note that female House Finch (p. 150) is streaked below; compare also with female Dickcissel (p. 146). House Sparrow often nests in eaves and gutters of homes and buildings. Call is an often-repeated *cheep*.

VINTER FINCHES AND HOUSE SPARROW

RED CROSSBILL

female

male

WHITE-WINGED
CROSSBILL

male

PINE GROSBEAK

female

male

EVENING GROSBEAK

female

male

summer male

HOUSE SPARROW

female

winter male

APPENDIX

FEEDING BIRDS

Putting up bird feeders is the best way to bring birds close to you—indeed, right up to your window. As they take turns plucking seeds from the tray or squabbling noisily over perching rights, you can study how birds move, as well as appreciate each species' unique feeding and social behavior.

Feeding birds can be as simple as scattering bread crumbs on the lawn or as involved as you want it to be. Many types of feeders are available from garden centers, mail-order outlets, and specialized stores catering just to birdwatchers. Homemade feeders are much cheaper and provide a fun and educational shared project for children and parents. Hopper-type feeders, which store seed in a tube or box, gradually dispensing it into a tray, are the most convenient to use. Just make sure that the hopper is weatherproof and easy to fill and clean.

Most people opt to fill their feeders with a commercially available seed mix. But as soon as the neighborhood birds have found your feeder, you will notice that each species seems to have its own seed preferences. By offering different types of seed in a number of different feeders, you can attract the widest variety of birds to your yard and minimize the amount of wasted seed.

The following table lists seed types and the birds each attracts:

Type of Seed	Birds Attracted
Sunflower	Chickadees, titmice, nuthatches, finches, grosbeaks, and jays
Niger (thistle)	Goldfinches, siskins, and other finches; chickadees and titmice
Millet	Juncos, sparrows, towhees, doves, jays, and blackbirds
Cracked corn	Blackbirds, sparrows, doves, pheasants, and other gamebirds

In northern climates, bird feeders may help some birds survive severe winters. The best high-energy food you can offer birds in winter is beef fat, or suet (available at the meat counters of most supermarkets). Suet will attract a variety of woodpeckers to your feeders, as well as chickadees, titmice, nuthatches, and jays. Hang suet chunks in plastic-mesh onion bags or in feeders crafted from wood and 1/2" hardware cloth. Peanut butter or a melted and resolidified blend of peanut butter and suet can be stuffed into 1" holes drilled in a hanging log or smeared into the cracks of a pinecone.

You can feed birds year-round, though it is best not to during the spring and summer, when plenty of natural food is available. At this time of year, birds need high-protein insect food for their nestlings.

During the spring and summer, you might want to shift to feeding hummingbirds. The Ruby-throated Hummingbird is a fairly common summer resident of rural communities throughout the East. It is very tame and readily visits feeders filled with a solution of clear sugar water (1 part sugar/4 parts water). Many adequate hummingbird feeders are commercially available. Make sure to buy one that is easy to clean.

POLE-MOUNTED
HOPPER FEEDER

hinged top

cone of galvanized
sheet metal to deter
squirrels

TUBE FEEDER FOR
SUNFLOWER
OR NIGER SEED

HOMEMADE
SODA BOTTLE
FEEDER

log with suet
packed into
1" drilled holes

dowel perch

1/2" hardware
cloth

sugar
water

HUMMINGBIRD
FEEDER

HOMEMADE
SUET FEEDERS

BIRDWATCHERS' CLUBS AND ORGANIZATIONS

Joining an organization of birdwatchers and participating in its field trips is one of the best ways for a novice to meet other enthusiasts and to learn from more experienced birders. The two national organizations listed below are geared especially for birdwatchers. Other environmental groups, such as the Sierra Club and Nature Conservancy, have state and regional chapters that may also sponsor bird walks. Local bird clubs and state and provincial ornithological societies are additional sources of birding expertise and companionship. Many provide the telephone numbers for "Rare Bird Alerts," which are up-to-date recordings of unusual sightings.

American Birding Association (P.O. Box 6599, Colorado Springs, CO 80934). The ABA publishes *Birding* magazine and *Winging It* newsletter, which feature articles on bird finding, identification, and taxonomy, as well as reviews of bird books and paraphernalia. The ABA also issues a directory of members, many of whom are available to assist fellow members in finding birds and planning field trips. ABA Sales offers optical equipment, computer software, field guides and other books—all at discount prices to members.

National Audubon Society (700 Broadway, New York, NY 10003). One of the oldest conservation organizations, the Audubon Society has chapters throughout the United States, which administer sanctuaries and environmental centers and sponsor field trips. The national organization publishes two magazines, *Audubon* and *American Birds*. *American Birds* features articles on bird identification and conservation, as well as seasonal reports of rare sightings. It also publishes the results of the annual Christmas Bird Counts.

MAGAZINES FOR BIRDERS

American Birds (quarterly). 700 Broadway, New York, NY 10003.

Birding (bimonthly). P.O. Box 6599, Colorado Springs, CO 80934.

Bird Watcher's Digest (bimonthly). P.O. Box 110, Marietta, OH 45750.

Birder's World (bimonthly). 720 East 8th Street, Holland, MI 49424.

The Living Bird Quarterly. Cornell Laboratory of Ornithology, 159 Sapsucker Woods Road, Ithaca, NY 14850.

WildBird (monthly). Fancy Publications, Inc., 3 Burroughs, Irving, CA 92718.

ADDITIONAL REFERENCES

Comprehensive North American Bird Guides

Farrand, John, Jr., ed. *Audubon Society Master Guide to Birding,* 3 vols. New York: Knopf, 1983.

Peterson, Roger Tory. *A Field Guide to the Birds,* 4th ed., 1980; *A Field Guide to the Birds of Texas and Adjacent States*, 1963. *A Field Guide to Western Birds,* 4th ed., 1990. All Boston: Houghton Mifflin.

Robbins, Chandler S., et al. *Birds of North America: A Guide to Field*

Identification, rev. ed. New York: Golden Press, 1983.

Scott, Shirley L., ed. *Field Guide to the Birds of North America,* 2nd ed. Washington, D.C.: National Geographic Society, 1987.

Advanced and Taxonomic Guides

Chandler, Richard J. *North Atlantic Shorebirds.* New York: Facts on File, 1989.

Clark, William S., and Brian K. Wheeler. *A Field Guide to the Hawks.* Boston: Houghton Mifflin, 1987.

Dunne, Pete, et al. *Hawks in Flight.* Boston: Houghton Mifflin,1988.

Grant, Peter J. *Gulls: A Guide to Identification,* rev. ed. Staffordshire, England: T. & A. D. Poyser, 1986.

Harrison, Peter. *Seabirds: An Identification Guide.* Beckenham, Kent, England: Croom Helm, 1983.

Hayman, Peter, et al. *Shorebirds: An Identification Guide.* Boston: Houghton Mifflin, 1986.

Kaufman, Kenn. *A Field Guide to Advanced Birding.* Boston: Houghton Mifflin, 1990.

Madge, Steve, and Hilary Burn. *Waterfowl.* Boston: Houghton Mifflin, 1988.

Bird Song Recordings

Cornell Laboratory of Ornithology. *A Field Guide to Bird Songs of Eastern and Central North America,* 3rd ed., 1990; *Western Bird Songs,* rev. ed., 1991. Both Boston: Houghton Mifflin.

Cornell Laboratory of Ornithology. *Guide to Bird Sounds.* Washington, D.C.: National Geographic Society, 1985.

Walton, Richard K., and Robert W. Lawson. *Birding by Ear: Guide to Bird Song Identification.* Boston: Houghton Mifflin, 1989.

Attracting Birds

Kress, Steven W. *The Audubon Society Guide to Attracting Birds.* New York: Scribners, 1985.

Terres, John K. *Songbirds in Your Garden,* 3rd ed. New York: Hawthorne, 1977.

Other Essential Reading

Austin, Oliver A., Jr. *Families of Birds: A Guide to Bird Classification,* rev. ed. New York: Golden Press, 1985.

Ehrlich, Paul R., et al. *The Birder's Handbook: A Field Guide to the Natural History of North American Birds.* New York: Simon & Schuster, 1988.

Gill, Frank B. *Ornithology.* New York: W. H. Freeman, 1990.

Terres, John K. *Audubon Society Encyclopedia of North American Birds.* New York: Knopf, 1980.

INDEX

Italicized page numbers refer to illustrations.

Accipiters, 50
Accipiter striatus, 50
Actitis macularia, 70
Aegolius acadicus, 88
Agelaius phoeniceus, 134
Aix sponsa, 36
Ajaia ajaja, 52
Ammodramus savannarum, 146
Anas
  acuta, 34
  americana, 36
  clypeata, 36
  crecca, 36
  discors, 36
  platyrhynchos, 34
  rubripes, 34
  strepera, 34
Anhinga, 30, *31*
Anhinga anhinga, 30
Ani
  Groove-billed, 84
  Smooth-billed, 84, *85*
Anser albifrons, 32
Anthus rubescens, 148
Aramus guarauna, 52
Archilochus colubris, 92
Ardea herodias, 58
Arenaria interpres, 64
Asio flammeus, 88
Avocet, American, *14*, 66, *67*
Aythya
  affinis, 38
  americana, 38
  collaris, 38
  valisineria, 38

Bartramia longicauda, 68
Birds of prey, 44-50
Birdwatching
  basics of, 6-11
  clubs and organizations, 156
Bittern(s), 54
  American, 54, *55*
  Least, 54, *55*
Blackbird(s), 134-136
  Brewer's, 136, *137*
  Red-winged, *19*, *25*, 134, *135*
  Rusty, 136, 137
  Yellow-headed, 134, 135
Bluebird
  Eastern, *18*, 116, *117*
  Mountain, 116, *117*
Bobolink, *25*, 134, *135*
Bobwhite, Northern, *18*, 60, *61*
Bombycilla cedrorum, 116
Bonasa umbellus, 60
Botaurus lentiginosus, 54
Brant, *12*, 32, *33*
Branta
  bernicla, 32
  canadensis, 32
Bubo virginianus, 86
Bubulcus ibis, 56
Bucephala
  albeola, 40
  clangula, 40
Bunting
  Indigo, *24*, 140, *141*
  Lark, *25*, 148, *149*
  Lazuli, 140, *141*
  Painted, *23*, 140, *141*
  Snow, 148, *149*
Buteo
  jamaicensis, 48
  lineatus, 48
  platypterus, 48
  swainsoni, 48
Buteos, 48
Butorides virescens, 54

Calamospiza melanocorys, 148
Calcarius ornatus, 148
Calidris

alba, 72
alpina, 72
canutus, 72
minutilla, 72
pusilla, 72
Camprimulgus vociferus, 90
Cardinal, Northern, *20*, 140, 141
Cardinalis cardinalis, 140
Carduelis
  flammea, 150
  pinus, 150
  tristis, 150
Carpodacus
  mexicanus, 150
  purpureus, 150
Casmerodius albus, 56
Catbird, Gray, *21*, 112, *113*
Cathartes aura, 44
Catharus
  fuscescens, 114
  guttatus, 114
  ustulatus, 114
Catoptrophorus semipalmatus, 70
Cepphus grylle, 28
Certhia americana, 108
Ceryle alcyon, 92
Chaetura pelagica, 90
Charadrius
  semipalmatus, 64
  vociferus, 64
Chat, Yellow-breasted, 120, *121*
Chen caerulescens, 32
Chickadee
  Black-capped, *20*, 106, *107*
  Boreal, 106, *107*
Chlidonias niger, 78
Chondestes grammacus, 146
Chordeiles minor, 90
Chuck-will's-widow, 90, *91*
Circus cyaneus, 46
Cistothorus palustris, 110
Clangula hyemalis, 42
Coccothraustes vespertinus, 152
Coccyzus
  americanus, 84
  erythropthalmus, 84
Colaptes auratus, 94
Colinus virginianus, 60
Columba livia, 82
Columbina passerina, 82
Contopus
  borealis, 100
  virens, 100
Coot, American, *13*, 62, *63*
Coragyps atratus, 44
Cormorant(s), 30
  Double-crested, *12*, *15*, 30, *31*
  Great, 30, *31*
  Neotropic, 30
Corvus
  brachyrhynchos, 104
  corax, 104
Cowbird, Brown-headed, *24*, 136, *137*
Crane
  Sandhill, *14*, 58, *59*
  Whooping, 58, *59*
Creeper, Brown, *20*, 108, *109*
Crossbill
  Red, 152, *153*
  White-winged, 152, *153*
Crotophaga ani, 84
Crow(s), 104
  American, *16*, *18*, 104, *105*
  Fish, 104
Cuckoo(s), 84
  Black-billed, 84, *85*
  Yellow-billed, 84, *85*
Curlew, Long-billed, 66, *67*
Cyanocitta cristata, 104
Cygnus columbianus, 32

Dendroica
  caerulescens, 128
  coronata, 132
  discolor, 124, 132

dominica, 126
fusca, 130
magnolia, 130
palmarum, 132
pensylvanica, 124
petechia, 124
pinus, 126, 132
virens, 130
Dickcissel, *24*, 146, *147*
Dolichonyx oryzivorus, 134
Dove(s), 82
  Common Ground-, 82, *83*
  Inca, 82, *83*
  Mourning, *18*, *20*, 82, *83*
  Rock, 82, *83*
  White-winged, 82, *83*
Dowitcher
  Long-billed, *14*, 68, *69*
  Short-billed, 68, *69*
Dryocopus pileatus, 92
Duck(s), dabbling, 34-36
  American Black, 34, *35*
  Gadwall, *12*, 34, *35*
  Mallard, 34, *35*
  Mottled, 34
  Northern Pintail, 34, *35*
  Northern Shoveler, 36, *37*
  Teal, Blue-winged, 36, *37*
  Teal, Green-winged, *12*, 36, *37*
  Wigeon, American, *12*, 36, *37*
  Wigeon, Eurasian, 36
  Wood, *12*, 36, *37*
Duck(s), diving, 38-42
  Bufflehead, *13*, 40, *41*
  Canvasback, 38, *39*
  Eider, Common, *13*, 42, *43*
  Eider, King, 42
  Goldeneye, Barrow's, 40
  Goldeneye, Common, *13*, 40, *41*
  Harlequin, 42
  Merganser, Common, 40, *41*
  Merganser, Hooded, *12*, 40, *41*
  Merganser, Red-breasted, *13*, 40, *41*
  Oldsquaw, *12*, 42, *43*
  Redhead, 38, *39*
  Ring-necked, *12*, 38, *39*
  Ruddy, *12*, 38, *39*
  Scaup, Greater, *13*, 38, *39*
  Scaup, Lesser, 38, *39*
  Scoter, Black, 42, *43*
  Scoter, Surf, *13*, 42, *43*
  Scoter, White-winged, 42, *43*
Dumetella carolinensis, 112
Dunlin, *15*, 72, *73*

Eagle
  Bald, *16*, 44, *45*
  Golden, 44
Egret(s), 54-56, *56*
  Cattle, 56, *57*
  Great, 56, *57*
  Reddish, 56
  Snowy, *15*, 56, *57*
Egretta
  caerulea, 56
  thula, 56
  tricolor, 56
Elanoides forficatus, 46
Empidonax minimus, 100
Eremophila alpestris, 148
Eudocimus albus, 52
Euphagus
  carolinus, 136
  cyanocephalus, 136
Falco
  columbarius, 50
  peregrinus, 50
  sparverius, 50
Falcon(s), 50
  American Kestrel, *19*, 50, *51*
  Merlin, 50, *51*

Peregrine, *16*, 50, *51*
Feeding of birds, 154-155
Finch
    House, *20*, *24*, 150, *151*
    Purple, *24*, 150, *151*
Finches, winter, 152
Flicker, Northern, *18*, *19*, 94, *95*
Flycatcher(s), 98-100
    Acadian, 100
    Great Crested, 98, *99*
    Least, *22*, 100, *101*
    Olive-sided, 100, *101*
    Scissor-tailed, *18*, 98, *99*
    Willow, 100, *101*
Fulica americana, 62

Gallinago gallinago, 68
Gallinula chloropus, 62
Gallinules
    Common, 62
    Purple, 62, *63*
Gamebirds, 58-60
Gannet, Northern, *17*, 28, *29*
Gavia immer, 26
Geococcyx californianus, 84
Geothlypis trichas, 124, 132
Gnatcatchers, 118
    Blue-gray, *22*, 118,*119*
Godwit, Marbled, 66, *67*
Goldfinch, American, *19*, *20*, *22*, 150, *151*
Goose
    Canada, *13*, 32, *33*
    Greater White-fronted, 32, *33*
    Snow, *13*, 32, *33*
Goshawk, Northern, 50
Grackle
    Boat-tailed, 136, *137*
    Common, *19*, *21*, 136, *137*
    Great-tailed, 136
Grebe(s), 26
    Eared, *12*, 26, *27*
    Horned, *12*, 26, *27*
    Pied-billed, *13*, 26, *27*
    Red-necked, 26
Grosbeak
    Black-headed, 140, *141*
    Blue, *24*, 140, *141*
    Evening, *20*, 152, *153*
    Pine, 152, *153*
    Rose-breasted, *21*, *24*, 140, *141*
Grouse
    Ruffed, 60, *61*
    Sharp-tailed, 60, *61*
    Spruce, 60
Grus canadensis, 58
Guillemot, Black, *12*, 28, *29*
Guiraca caerulea, 140
Gull(s), 74-76
    Bonaparte's, *12*, 76, *77*
    California, 74
    Franklin's, *13*, 76, *77*
    Glaucous, 74
    Great Black-backed, *17*, 74, *75*
    Herring, *12*, *17*, 74, *75*
    Iceland, 74
    Laughing, *15*, *17*, 76, *77*
    Ring-billed, 74, *75*

Haematopus palliatus, 66
Haliaeetus leucocephalus, 44
Harrier, Northern, *16*, 46, *47*
Hawk
    Broad-winged, 48, *49*
    Cooper's, *16*, 50, 51
    Red-shouldered, 48, *49*
    Red-tailed, *16*, *18*, 48, *49*
    Rough-legged, *16*, 48, *49*
    Sharp-shinned, 50, *51*
    Swainson's, 48, *49*
Helmitheros vermivorus, 128
Heron(s), 54-58
    Black-crowned Night-, *15*, *17*, 54, *55*
    Great Blue, *15*, *16*, 58, *59*
    Green, *15*, 54, *55*
    Little Blue, 56, *57*
    Tricolored, 56, *57*

Yellow-crowned Night- 54, *55*
Himantopus mexicanus, 66
Hirundo
    pyrrhonota, 102
    rustica, 102
Hummingbird, Ruby-throated, *21*, 92, *93*
Hylocichla mustelina, 114

Ibis
    Glossy, 52, *53*
    White, 52, *53*
    White-faced, *14*, 52
Icteria virens, 120
Icterus
    galbula, 138
    spurius, 138
Ictinia mississippiensis, 46
Ixobrychus exilis, 54

Jay(s), 104
    Blue, *20*, 104, *105*
    Gray, 104, *105*
    Scrub, 104, *105*
Junco, Dark-eyed, *20*, 142, *143*
Junco hyemalis, 142

Kingbird
    Eastern, *19*, 98, *99*
    Gray, 98, *99*
    Western, 98, *99*
Kingfisher, Belted, *18*, 92, *93*
Kinglet(s), 118
    Golden-crowned, 118, *119*
    Ruby-crowned, *22*, 118, *119*
Kite
    American Swallow-tailed, 46, *47*
    Mississippi, 46, *47*
    Snail, 46
Kittiwake, Black-legged, 76, *77*
Knot, Red, 72, *73*

Lanius ludovicianus, 112
Larus
    argentatus, 74
    atricilla, 76
    delawarensis, 74
    marinus, 74
    philadelphia, 76
    pipixcan, 76
Limnodromus griseus, 68
Limosa fedoa, 66
Limpkin, 52, *53*
Longspur
    Chestnut-collared, 148, *149*
    Lapland, 140, *149*
Loon(s), 26
    Common, *12*, 26, *27*
    Red-throated, 26, *27*
Lophodytes cucullatus, 40
Loxia curvirostra, 152

Magpie, Black-billed, 104, *105*
Martin, Purple, 102, *103*
Meadowlark
    Eastern, *19*, 134, *135*
    Western, 134
Melanerpes
    carolinus, 94
    erythrocephalus, 94
Melanitta
    fusca, 42
    perspicillata, 42
Meleagris gallopavo, 58
Melospiza
    georgiana, 144
    melodia, 144
Mergus
    merganser, 40
    serrator, 40
Mimus polyglottos, 112
Mniotilta varia, 128
Mockingbird, Northern, *21*, 112, *113*
Molothrus ater, 136
Moorhen, Common, *14*, 62, *63*
Mycteria americana, 52
Myiarchus crinitus, 98

Nighthawk, Common, *19*, 90, *91*
Nightjars, 90
Numenius phaeopus, 66
Nuthatch(es), 108
    Brown-headed, 108, *109*
    Red-breasted, 108, *109*
    White-breasted, *20*, 108, *109*
Nyctanassa violacea, 54
Nyctea scandiaca, 86
Nycticorax nycticorax, 54

Oceanites oceanicus, 28
Oriole
    Northern, *21*, 138, *139*
    Orchard, *22*, 138, *139*
Osprey, *17*, 46, *47*
Otus asio, 88
Ovenbird, *25*, 128, *129*
Owl(s), 86-88
    Barn, 86, *87*
    Barred, 86, *87*
    Burrowing, 88, *89*
    Eastern Screech-, 88, *89*
    Great Horned, 86, *87*
    Long-eared, 88, *89*
    Northern Saw-whet, 88, *89*
    Short-eared, *16*, 88, *89*
    Snowy, *17*, 86, *87*
Oxyura jamaicensis, 38
Oystercatcher, American, *14*, 66, *67*

Pandion haliaetus, 46
Partridge, Gray, 60, *61*
Parula, Northern, *22*, 126, *127*, 132, *133*
Parula americana, 126, 132
Parus
    atricapillus, 106
    bicolor, 106
    carolinensis, 106
Passerculus sandwichensis, 146
Passer domesticus, 152
Passerella iliaca, 144
Passerina
    ciris, 140
    cyanea, 140
Pelecanus
    erythrorhynchos, 30
    occidentalis, 30
Pelican(s), 30
    American White, *13*, 30, *31*
    Brown, 30, 31
Perdix perdix, 60
Perisoreus canadensis, 104
Pewee, Eastern Wood-, 100, *101*
Phalacrocorax auritus, 30
Phalarope, Wilson's, *13*, 70, *71*
Phalaropus tricolor, 70
Phasianus colchicus, 60
Pheasant, Ring-necked, 60, *61*
Pheucticus ludovicianus, 140
Phoebe
    Eastern, *23*, 100, *101*
    Say's, 100
Pica pica, 104
Picoides
    pubescens, 96
    villosus, 96
Pigeon(s), 82
    Domestic, 82
    White-crowned, 82, *83*
Pinicola enucleator, 152
Pipilo erythrophthalmus, 142
Pipit, American, *25*, 148, *149*
Piranga
    olivacea, 138
    rubra, 138
Plectrophenax nivalis, 148
Plegadis falcinellus, 52
Plover(s), 64
    American Golden-, 64, *65*
    Black-bellied, *15*, 64, *65*
    Killdeer, *14*, *19*, 64, *65*
    Piping, 64, *65*
    Semipalmated, *15*, 64, *65*
Pluvialis squatarola, 64

Podiceps
  auritus, 26
  nigricollis, 26
Podilymbus podiceps, 26
Polioptila caerulea, 118
Pooecetes gramineus, 146
Porzana carolina, 62
Prairie-Chicken
  Greater, 60
  Lesser, 60
Progne subis, 102
Protonotaria citrea, 126
Puffinis gravis, 28

Quail, Scaled, 60
Quiscalus
  major, 136
  quiscula, 136

Rail(s), 62
  Clapper, *15*, 62, *63*
  King, 62
  Sora, *14*, 62, *63*
  Virginia, 62, *63*
Rallus
  limicola, 62
  longirostris, 62
Raptors, 44-50
Raven, Common, 104, *105*
Recurvirostra americana, 66
Redpoll, Common, 150, *151*
Redstart, American, 128, *129*
Regulus
  calendula, 118
  satrapa, 118
Riparia riparia, 102
Rissa tridactyla, 76
Roadrunner, Greater, 84, *85*
Robin, American, *18*, *21*, 116, *117*
Rynchops niger, 80

Sanderling, 72, *73*
Sandpiper
  Least, 72, *73*
  Purple, 72
  Semipalmated, 72, *73*
  Solitary, 70, *71*
  Spotted, *15*, 70, *71*
  Upland, 68, *69*
  Western, 72
Sapsucker, Yellow-bellied, 96, *97*
Sayornis phoebe, 100
Scolopax minor, 68
Seabirds, 28
Seiurus
  aurocapillus, 128
  motacilla, 128
Setophaga ruticilla, 128
Shearwater
  Greater, *17*, 28, *29*
  Sooty, 28
Shorebirds, 66-72
Shrike
  Loggerhead, 112, *113*
  Northern, 112
Sialia sialis, 116
Siskin, Pine, *24*, 150, *151*
Sitta
  canadensis, 108
  carolinensis, 108
  pusilla, 108
Skimmer, Black, *14*, *17*, 80, *81*
Snipe, Common, *14*, 68, *69*
Somateria mollissima, 42
Sparrow
  American Tree, 142, *143*
  Chipping, *21*, *24*, 142, *143*
  Clay-colored, 142, *143*
  Field, 142, *143*
  Fox, *25*, 144, *145*
  Grasshopper, *25*, 146, *147*
  Harris', 144, *145*
  House, *20*, *24*, 152, *153*
  Lark, 146, *147*
  Savannah, 146, *147*
  Sharp-tailed, 146, *147*
  Song, *21*, *24*, 144, *145*
  Swamp, 144, *145*

Vesper, *25*, 146, *147*
  White-crowned, 144, *145*
  White-throated, *20*, 144, *145*
Speotyto cunicularia, 88
Sphyrapicus varius, 96
Spiza americana, 146
Spizella
  arborea, 142
  passerina, 142
  pusilla, 142
Spoonbill, Roseate, 52, *53*
Starling, European, *21*, 136, *137*
Sterna
  antillarum, 78
  caspia, 80
  forsteri, 78
  hirundo, 78
  maxima, 80
  nilotica, 80
Stilt, Black-necked, *14*, 66, *67*
Stork, Wood, 52, *53*
Storm-Petrel, Wilson's, 28, *29*
Strix varia, 86
Sturnella magna, 134
Sturnus vulgaris, 136
Sula bassanus, 28
Swallow(s), 102
  Bank, 102, *103*
  Barn, *18*, 102, *103*
  Cliff, 102, *103*
  Northern Rough-winged, 102, *103*
  Tree, *18*, 102, *103*
Swan
  Mute, 32, *33*
  Tundra, *13*, 32, *33*
Swift, Chimney, *21*, 90, *91*

Tachycineta bicolor, 102
Tanager(s), 138
  Scarlet, *23*, 138, *139*
  Summer, 138, *139*
Tern(s), 78-80
  Black, 78, *79*
  Caspian, *17*, 80, *81*
  Common, *14*, *17*, 78, *79*
  Forster's, 78, *79*
  Gull-billed, 80, *81*
  Least, 78, *79*
  Roseate, 78
  Royal, 80, *81*
  Sandwich, 80, *81*
Thrasher, Brown, *21*, 112, *113*
Thrush(es), 114-116
  Gray-cheeked, 114, *115*
  Hermit, *25*, 114, *115*
  Swainson's, 114, *115*
  Wood, *21*, 114, *115*
Thrushes, mimic, 112
Thryomanes bewickii, 110
Thryothorus ludovicianus, 110
Titmouse-mice, 106
  Tufted, *20*, 106, *107*
Towhee, Rufous-sided, *21*, 142, *143*
Toxostoma rufum, 112
Tringa
  melanoleuca, 70
  solitaria, 70
Troglodytes aedon, 110
Turdus migratorius, 116
Turkey, Wild, 58, *59*
Turnstone, Ruddy, *14*, 64, *65*
Tympanuchus phasianellus, 60
Tyrannus
  forficatus, 98
  tyrannus, 98
  verticalis, 98
Tyto alba, 86

Veery, 114, *115*
Vermivora
  celata, 132
  pinus, 124
  ruficapilla, 130
Vireo(s), 118-120
  Bell's, 120, *121*
  Red-eyed, 118, *119*
  Solitary, 120, *121*
  Warbling, *23*, 118, *119*

White-eyed, *22*, 120, *121*
  Yellow-throated, 120, *121*
Vireo
  bellii, 120
  flavifrons, 120
  griseus, 120
  olivaceous, 118
  solitarius, 120
Vulture
  Black, 44, *45*
  Turkey, *16*, 44, *45*

Warbler
  Black-and-white, 128, *129*
  Blackburnian, 130, *131*
  Black-throated Blue, *23*, 128, *129*
  Black-throated Green, 130, *131*
  Blue-winged, 124, *125*
  Canada, 130, *131*
  Cerulean, 126, *127*
  Chestnut-sided, *22*, 124, *125*
  Golden-winged, 124, *125*
  Hooded, 126, *127*
  Kentucky, 126, *127*
  Magnolia, 130, *131*
  Nashville, 130, *131*
  Orange-crowned, *23*, 132, *133*
  Palm, *25*, 132, *133*
  Pine, *22*, 126, *127*
  Prairie, 124, *125*, 132, *133*
  Prothonotary, 126, *127*
  Worm-eating, 128, *129*
  Yellow, *22*, 124, *125*
  Yellow-rumped, 130, *131*, 132, *133*
  Yellow-throated, 126, *127*
Waterfowl, 32. See also Duck(s), dabbling; Duck(s), diving; Goose; Swan
Waterthrush
  Louisiana, *25*, 128, *129*
  Northern, 128, *129*
Waxwing
  Bohemian, 116
  Cedar, *20*, 116, *117*
Whimbrel, *15*, 66, *67*
Whip-poor-will, 90, *91*
Willet, *14*, 70, *71*
Wilsonia
  canadensis, 130
  citrina, 126
Woodcock, American, 68, *69*
Woodpecker(s), 92-96
  Black-backed, 96, *97*
  Downy, *20*, 96, *97*
  Golden-fronted, 94, *95*
  Hairy, 96, *97*
  Ladder-backed, 96, *97*
  Pileated, 92, *93*
  Red-bellied, 94, *95*
  Red-headed, *19*, 94, *95*
  Three-toed, 96
Wood-warblers, 122. See also Warbler
Wren(s), 110
  Bewick's, 110, *111*
  Carolina, *20*, 110, *111*
  House, *23*, 110, *111*
  Marsh, 110, *111*
  Sedge, 110
  Winter, 110, *111*

Xanthocephalus xanthocephalus, 134

Yellowlegs
  Greater, 70, *71*
  Lesser, *15*, 70, *71*
Yellowthroat, Common, *21*, *23*, 124, *125*, 132, *133*

Zenaida macroura, 82
Zonotrichia
  albicollis, 144
  leucophrysa, 144